THE BRONTËS
AT HAWORTH

THE BRONTËS AT HAWORTH

ANN DINSDALE

PHOTOGRAPHS BY SIMON WARNER

F

FRANCES LINCOLN LIMITED
PUBLISHERS
www.franceslincoln.com

To my children, Emily and Joe

Frances Lincoln Ltd
4 Torriano Mews
Torriano Avenue
London NW5 2RZ
www.franceslincoln.com

The Brontës at Haworth
Copyright © Frances Lincoln 2006
Text copyright © Ann Dinsdale 2006
Archive photographs copyright © the Brontë Parsonage Museum
and all other photographs copyright © Simon Warner (as listed in the
acknowledgements on page 160)

First Frances Lincoln edition: 2006

A catalogue record for this book is available from the British Library.

ISBN 10 0-7112-2572-9
ISBN 13 978-0-7112-2572-5

Printed and bound in Singapore

9 8 7 6 5 4 3 2 1

PAGE 1 *This ambrotype photograph is the earliest known image
of Haworth Parsonage. It was taken from the tower of the Old
Church and shows the house as it would have looked in the
Brontës' time.*

PAGE 2 *Charlotte Bronte's paint box and her watercolour study
of a heartsease.*

CONTENTS

THE BRONTËS: A CHRONOLOGY

YEAR	EVENT
1777, 17 March	Patrick Brontë is born at Emdale, County Down, Ireland
1783, 15 April	Maria Branwell is born at Penzance, Cornwall
1802	Patrick Brontë enters St John's College, Cambridge
1806	Patrick Brontë is ordained as a clergyman in the Church of England
1806–1809	Patrick Brontë is appointed Curate at Wethersfield, Essex
1809, January–December	Patrick Brontë is appointed Curate at Wellington, Shropshire
1809, December–1811	Patrick Brontë is appointed Curate at Dewsbury, Yorkshire
1811–15	Patrick Brontë is appointed Minister at Hartshead-cum-Clifton, Yorkshire
1812	Maria Branwell visits her uncle, John Fennell, headmaster of Woodhouse Grove School, near Bradford, where Patrick is an examiner in the classics
1812, 29 December	Patrick Brontë marries Maria Branwell at Guisley Church, near Leeds
1814	Maria Brontë is born at Hartshead. Baptized at Hartshead on 23 April
1815, 8 February	Elizabeth Brontë is born at Hartshead. Baptized at Thornton, near Bradford, on 26 August
1815	Patrick Brontë is appointed Perpetual Curate at Thornton, near Bradford

YEAR	EVENT
1816, 21 April	Charlotte Brontë is born at Thornton. Baptized at Thornton on 29 June
1817, 26 June	Patrick Branwell Brontë is born at Thornton. Baptized at Thornton on 23 July
1818, 30 July	Emily Jane Brontë is born at Thornton. Baptized at Thornton on 20 August
1820, 17 January	Anne Brontë is born at Thornton. Baptized at Thornton on 25 March
1820, February	Patrick Brontë is appointed Perpetual Curate at Haworth, near Bradford in West Yorkshire
1820, April	The Brontë family moves to Haworth Parsonage
1821, 15 September	Mrs Brontë dies and is buried in Haworth Church; her sister, Miss Elizabeth Branwell, comes from Penzance to look after the family
1824, July	Maria and Elizabeth are sent to the Clergy Daughters' School at Cowan Bridge, Kirkby Lonsdale. They are joined in August by Charlotte and in November by Emily
1825, 6 May	Maria dies at Haworth, having left school because of ill health on 14 February
1825, 1 June	Charlotte and Emily are withdrawn from school
1825, 15 June	Elizabeth dies at Haworth, having left school because of ill health on 31 May

YEAR	EVENT
1825	Tabitha Aykroyd comes as a servant to the Parsonage at Haworth
1831, January	Charlotte goes to Miss Wooler's school at Roe Head, Mirfield, near Dewsbury, where she meets Ellen Nussey and Mary Taylor
1832, June	Charlotte leaves Roe Head to teach her sisters at home
1835, July	Charlotte returns to Roe Head as a teacher, taking Emily as a pupil; Emily stays only briefly and is replaced by Anne, who stays till December 1837
1838, June	Branwell sets up as a portrait painter in Bradford. He returns home in debt in May 1839
1838, September	Emily works as teacher at Miss Patchett's school at Law Hill, near Halifax, where she stays approximately six months
1838, December	Charlotte leaves her teaching post at Roe Head
1839, April–December	Anne works as a governess for Mrs Ingham at Blake Hall, Mirfield
1839, May–July	Charlotte works as a governess for Mrs Sidgwick at Stonegappe, Lothersdale, in North Yorkshire
1839, August	William Weightman is appointed Curate at Haworth Church
1839, September	Charlotte and Ellen Nussey take a holiday at Easton Farm, Bridlington, on the Yorkshire coast
1840, January–June	Branwell works as tutor for Mr Postlethwaite at Broughton-in-Furness in the Lake District

YEAR	EVENT
1840, May	Anne works as a governess for Mrs Robinson at Thorp Green Hall, Little Ouseburn, near York
1840, October	Branwell works as clerk on the Leeds–Manchester railway at Sowerby Bridge, Halifax
1841, March–December	Charlotte works as a governess for Mrs White at Upperwood House, Rawdon, near Leeds
1841, April	Branwell is promoted and sent as clerk-in-charge to Luddenden Foot, near Halifax
1842, February	Charlotte and Emily travel to Brussels to study at the Pensionnat Heger
1842, April	Branwell is dismissed from his post at Luddenden Foot for negligence in keeping the accounts
1842, 6 September	William Weightman dies, aged twenty-six, and is buried in Haworth Church
1842, 29 October	Miss Elizabeth Branwell dies, aged sixty-six, and is buried in Haworth Church. On the death of their aunt, Charlotte and Emily are recalled from Brussels
1843, January	Charlotte returns to Brussels. Emily remains at Haworth Parsonage as housekeeper. Branwell joins Anne at Thorp Green as tutor to Edmund Robinson
1844, January	Charlotte leaves Brussels and returns home
1845, May	Arthur Bell Nicholls is appointed Curate at Haworth Church
1845, June	Anne resigns from her post at Thorp Green

YEAR	EVENT
1845, July	Branwell is dismissed from Thorp Green. Charlotte stays with Ellen Nussey at Hathersage, Derbyshire
1846, May	*Poems by Currer, Ellis and Acton Bell* is published by Aylott and Jones at the sisters' expense
1846, June	Charlotte completes *The Professor*, which is rejected by several publishers. By July Emily has completed *Wuthering Heights* and Anne *Agnes Grey*
1846, August	Charlotte accompanies her father to Manchester for a cataract operation and begins writing *Jane Eyre*
1847, 19 October	*Jane Eyre* is published by Smith, Elder & Co. under Charlotte's pseudonym, Currer Bell
1847, December	*Wuthering Heights* and *Agnes Grey* are published together by Thomas Cautley Newby under Emily and Anne's pseudonyms, Ellis and Acton Bell
1848, June	*The Tenant of Wildfell Hall*, Anne's second novel, is published by Thomas Cautley Newby
1848, July	Charlotte and Anne travel to London to prove to Smith, Elder & Co. that they are separate individuals after Newby claims that the Bells are a single author
1848, 24 September	Branwell dies, aged thirty-one, and is buried in Haworth Church
1848, 19 December	Emily dies, aged thirty, and is buried in Haworth Church

YEAR	EVENT
1849, 28 May	Anne dies, aged twenty-nine, and is buried in St Mary's churchyard at Scarborough, where she had gone in the hope of a sea cure
1849, June	Charlotte stays at Filey and at Easton Farm, Bridlington, on the Yorkshire coast
1849, 26 October	*Shirley* is published by Smith, Elder & Co. under Charlotte's pseudonym, Currer Bell
1849, December	Charlotte stays with George Smith's family in London, where she meets W.M. Thackeray and Harriet Martineau
1850, March	Charlotte visits Sir James Kay-Shuttleworth at Gawthorpe Hall, near Burnley
1850, June	Charlotte stays with the Smith family in London, dining with Thackeray and having her portrait painted by George Richmond
1850, July	Charlotte visits Edinburgh with George Smith
1850, August	Charlotte stays with the Kay-Shuttleworths at Briery Close, Windermere, where she meets Elizabeth Gaskell
1850, December	Charlotte visits Harriet Martineau at the Knoll, Ambleside
1851, May–June	Charlotte visits London, sees the Great Exhibition and attends Thackeray's lectures
1851, June	Charlotte stays with Elizabeth Gaskell at Plymouth Grove, Manchester

YEAR	EVENT	YEAR	EVENT
1852, June	Charlotte stays alone at Filey and visits Anne's grave at Scarborough	1855, January	Charlotte and Mr Nicholls visit the Kay-Shuttleworths at Gawthorpe Hall. Charlotte catches a cold from walking on the wet grass from which she never fully recovers
1852, December	Arthur Bell Nicholls proposes marriage to Charlotte but is rejected because of her father's objections	1855, 17 February	Tabitha Aykroyd dies, aged eighty-four, and is buried in Haworth churchyard
1853, January	Charlotte visits London for the last time. *Villette* is published by Smith, Elder & Co. under Charlotte's pseudonym, Currer Bell	1855, 31 March	Charlotte dies, aged thirty-eight, in the early stages of pregnancy
1853, April	Charlotte stays with Elizabeth Gaskell at Plymouth Grove, Manchester	1857, March	*The Life of Charlotte Brontë* by Elizabeth Gaskell is published by Smith, Elder & Co.
1853, May	Arthur Bell Nicholls resigns his curacy at Haworth. In August he transfers to Kirk Smeaton, Pontefract	1857, June	*The Professor*, Charlotte's first novel, is published by Smith, Elder & Co.
1853, September	Elizabeth Gaskell spends four days at Haworth Parsonage	1861, 7 June	Mr Brontë dies, aged eighty-four. Mr Nicholls leaves Haworth Parsonage and returns to Ireland
1854, January	Arthur Bell Nicholls stays with Mr Grant, Curate at Oxenhope, near Haworth, and meets Charlotte several times	1879	Haworth Church is demolished, except for the tower, and rebuilt on the same site
1854 April	Mr Brontë withdraws his objections to the marriage and Charlotte's engagement to Mr Nicholls is announced	1880, 19 January	Martha Brown, the Brontës' servant dies, aged fifty-two
1854, June	Arthur Bell Nicholls resumes his duties as Curate at Haworth	1893, 16 December	The Brontë Society is founded at a meeting in Bradford Town Hall
1854, 29 June	Charlotte and Arthur Bell Nicholls are married in Haworth Church by the Reverend Sutcliffe Sowden. Miss Wooler gives Charlotte away and Ellen Nussey acts as bridesmaid	1895, 18 May	The Brontë Museum is opened on the upper floor of the Yorkshire Penny Bank, Haworth
		1897, 26 November	Ellen Nussey dies, aged eighty
		1906, 2 December	Mr Nicholls dies at Banagher, Ireland, aged eighty-eight
1854, July	Charlotte and Mr Nicholls go on honeymoon to Ireland and visit Nicholls' relations	1928, 4 August	Haworth Parsonage is opened to the public as the Brontë Parsonage Museum, having been bought by Sir James Roberts and presented to the Brontë Society

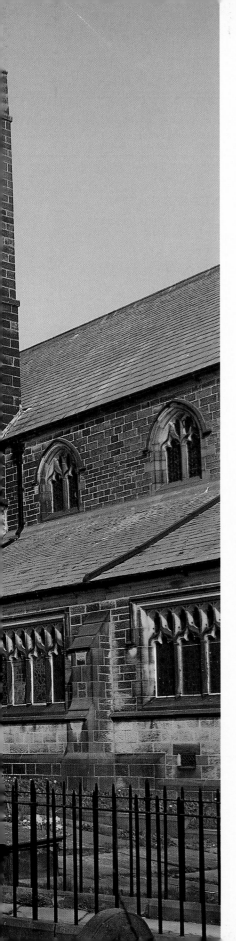

THE
BRONTË
FAMILY

ABOVE *This waterfall on Haworth Moor was a favoured spot for the Brontë children.*

LEFT *Haworth Church and the Brontë Parsonage Museum.*

11

PATRICK BRONTË

I have no objection whatever to your representing me as a LITTLE *eccentric, since you and your learned friends would have it so; only don't set me on in my fury to burning hearthrugs, sawing the backs off chairs, and tearing my wife's silk gowns … Had I been numbered amongst the calm,* CONCENTRIC *men of the world, I should not have been as I now am, and I should in all probability never have had such children as mine have been.*

PATRICK BRONTË, letter to Mrs Gaskell, 1855

In *The Life of Charlotte Brontë*, Mrs Gaskell wrote an account of Patrick Brontë's early life:

> The Rev. Patrick Brontë is a native of the County Down in Ireland. His father, Hugh Brontë, was left an orphan at an early age. He came from the south to the north of the island, and settled in the parish of Ahaderg, near Loughbrickland. There was some family tradition that, humble as Hugh Brontë's circumstances were, he was the descendant of an ancient family. But about this neither he nor his descendants have cared to inquire. He made an early marriage and reared and educated ten children on the proceeds of the few acres of land which he farmed. This large family were remarkable for great physical beauty. Even in his old age, Mr Brontë is a striking-looking man, above the common height, with a nobly-shaped head, and erect carriage. In his youth he must have been unusually handsome.

The family's original name is uncertain and appears in surviving records as 'Brunty', 'Prunty' and 'Bruntee'.

Patrick Brontë showed an 'early fondness for books', and at the age of sixteen he took the remarkable step of opening his own school. His ability attracted the attention of Thomas Tighe, a clergyman and Cambridge graduate, who employed Patrick Brontë as tutor to his children. It is not known when Patrick first decided on a career in the Church, but clearly Tighe was influential. He coached Patrick in the classics and prepared him for university.

Patrick entered St John's College, Cambridge, in 1802, and it was here that he changed his name from Brunty to the unique and more impressive-sounding Brontë. Various reasons have been suggested for the name change, one of them being that he was emulating his hero, Nelson, who had been created Duke of Brontë in 1799. Brontë is also the Greek word for thunder – an apt choice of name for an ambitious young man at the start of his career. Throughout his life Patrick Brontë used a variety of accents above the 'e' of his surname, but when he began to publish collections of prose and poetry, his printers made use of a diaresis instead, and this was the variation his children adopted.

Patrick held an assisted place at university as a sizar, for which he would have been expected to coach some of the wealthier undergraduates. His remarkable ability once again attracted attention, and several influential people, including William Wilberforce, sponsored Patrick's academic career. He clearly saw education as his best means of advancement and worked hard throughout his years at university, graduating in 1806.

Following ordination, Patrick held curacies at Wethersfield in Essex, and then Wellington in Shropshire, before heading north to Dewsbury in Yorkshire in 1809. In 1811 he was promoted to the living at Hartshead-cum-Clifton, also in Yorkshire, and during his time there acted as examiner in the classics at Woodhouse Grove School. It was here in 1812 that Patrick met Maria Branwell, daughter of a prosperous Cornish merchant, who was visiting her uncle, the school's headmaster.

The couple were married on 29 December 1812 at Guiseley Church, near Leeds, and at first may have set up home at Patrick's lodgings at Lousy Thorn Farm, before moving to Clough House in the village of Hightown. During Patrick's time at Hartshead, the couple's eldest daughters, Maria and Elizabeth, were born. Shortly after Elizabeth's birth Patrick was appointed Perpetual Curate of Thornton, near Bradford, and the family moved into the Parsonage on Market Street in 1815. It was here that the four famous Brontë children were born in quick succession – Charlotte (1816), Patrick Branwell (1817), Emily Jane (1818) and

ABOVE *A portrait of Patrick Brontë as a young man, by an unknown artist.*

BELOW *A plaque on the wall of the old Parsonage at Thornton, where the four younger Brontë children were born.*

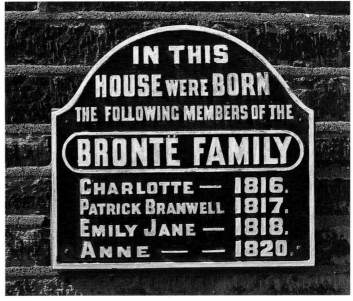

IN THIS HOUSE WERE BORN THE FOLLOWING MEMBERS OF THE BRONTË FAMILY

CHARLOTTE — 1816.
PATRICK BRANWELL 1817.
EMILY JANE — 1818.
ANNE — — 1820.

Anne (1820) – before the family moved to Haworth in 1820 upon Patrick's appointment as Perpetual Curate. This turned out to be the final move in Patrick's career. Although his salary was not large, he had come a long way from the crofter's cabin in Ireland: in an age of rigidly enforced class divisions, he had become a respected, middle-class clergyman.

Within eighteen months of the family's arrival at Haworth, Mrs Brontë died, and at the age of forty-four, Patrick found himself a widower with six young children on his hands. Medical fees had left him in debt and he missed the friends of Thornton days, finding himself 'a stranger in a strange land'. Kind friends came forward with loans to cover the nursing costs, and his wife's elder sister, Elizabeth Branwell, took charge of the running of the Parsonage at Haworth and the care of Patrick's children. The arrangement was intended to be a temporary one, but after Patrick had made three unsuccessful attempts to remarry, she remained at Haworth with the Brontë family.

Patrick Brontë had no independent income and it was always clear that his family would have to support themselves. After the deaths of his eldest daughters he kept his remaining family close by him at Haworth. He gave the children lessons at home and much has been written about Mr Brontë's enlightened attitude towards education. At a time when too much learning for girls was seen as unnecessary, he encouraged all his children in their eager pursuit of knowledge, and was later to tell Mrs Gaskell: 'I frequently thought I discovered signs of rising talent which I had seldom, or never before, seen in any of their age.' With this conviction, Mr Brontë was prepared to make financial sacrifices to enable his children to develop their talents. Emily and Anne received music lessons, and it is believed that all the children had drawing lessons from a local artist. Later,

COTTAGE POEMS,

BY THE

REV. PATRICK BRONTË, B. A.

MINISTER

OF

HARTSHEAD-CUM-CLIFTON,

NEAR LEEDS, YORKSHIRE.

All you who turn the sturdy soil,
Or ply the loom with daily toil,
And lowly on, through life turmoil
For scanty fare:
Attend: and gather richest spoil,
To sooth your care.

Halifax:

Printed and sold by P. K. Holden, for the Author.

Sold also by B. Crosby and Co. Stationers' Court, London;
F. Houlston and Son, Wellington;
and by the Booksellers of Halifax, Leeds, York, &c,

1811.

Mr Brontë paid the substantial sum of two guineas a week to the eminent Leeds artist William Robinson to instruct Branwell in the art of painting in oils.

During his early years as a curate, Mr Brontë had published collections of poetry and prose. These works were written to offer moral guidance to the less well educated and, although not great literature, they meant that Patrick's children grew up accustomed to the sight of books carrying their family name on the Parsonage shelves. Mr Brontë's rags-to-riches story must have made a profound impression

OPPOSITE *Patrick Brontë's* COTTAGE POEMS, *published in 1811 during his time at Hartshead.*

RIGHT *One of the several photographs of Patrick Brontë taken late in his life. When Mrs Gaskell visited the Parsonage in 1853, she described Mr Brontë as 'very polite and agreeable to me, paying rather elaborate old-fashioned compliments, but I was sadly afraid of him in my inmost soul; for I caught a glare of his stern eyes over his spectacles at Miss Brontë once or twice which made me know my man'.*

on the minds of his children. For Branwell, his father proved a hard act to follow, while for Charlotte, her father's example acted as a spur to literary ambition.

When Mrs Gaskell first met Patrick Brontë, he was in his seventies and had lost his wife and all but one of his six children. His mingled pride in Charlotte's fame and fear of losing her had left him a difficult and demanding father. Mrs Gaskell's perception of Mr Brontë, however, had already been formed three years before she met him, influenced by the gossipy accounts of Lady Kay-Shuttleworth at whose Windermere home she had first met Charlotte and fed by the tales of a dismissed servant; and she never checked the veracity of these stories concerning his strange

LEFT *A sample of Charlotte Brontë's handwriting, authenticated by her father. After her death, Mr Brontë cut Charlotte's letters into snippets to meet the many requests for samples of her handwriting that came from admirers of her books.*

OPPOSITE *The nearby village of Stanbury fell within Mr Brontë's far-flung parish.*

PATRICK BRONTË

habits. Mrs Gaskell described Mr Brontë as a 'wayward eccentric wild father' whom she held to be largely responsible for the 'peculiar circumstances' of Charlotte's upbringing. As a result, her *Life of Charlotte Brontë* gave rise to many myths concerning Mr Brontë, who emerges as a distant and rather frightening figure.

After Charlotte's death, Mr Brontë lived on at the Parsonage for six years, cared for by her widower, Arthur Bell Nicholls. He died there on Friday 7 June 1861 at the age of eighty-four. Although his own literary ambitions were never fulfilled, it was clearly a matter of great pride to Patrick Brontë that he became the father of genius.

MARIA BRANWELL

*Charlotte tried hard, in after years, to recall the remembrance of her mother, and
could bring back two or three pictures of her. One was when, sometime in the evening
light, she had been playing with her little boy, Patrick Branwell, in the parlour
of Haworth Parsonage. But the recollections of four or five years old are of a very
fragmentary character.*

ELIZABETH GASKELL, *The Life of Charlotte Brontë*, 1857

Mrs Brontë remains a shadowy figure in the Brontë story, for she died at the age of thirty-eight, when the eldest of her six children, Maria, was just seven years of age and the youngest, Anne, was still a babe in arms.

Maria Branwell grew up in a totally different world from that of Patrick Brontë. She was born on 15 April 1783, one of the seven surviving children of Thomas Branwell and his wife Anne Carne. Her father was a successful merchant and property owner, while her mother was the daughter of a prosperous silversmith. The Branwell family home was an elegant house in Chapel Street, Penzance, which in Maria's day was a thriving market town possessing a Ladies' Book Club, concert rooms and Assembly Rooms where balls were held throughout the winter months. Early in 1812, following the deaths of her parents, the twenty-nine-year-old Maria travelled to Yorkshire to visit to her aunt and uncle. Mrs Gaskell describes her at this time as 'extremely small in person; not pretty, but very elegant, and always dressed with a quiet simplicity of taste, which accorded well with her general character, and of which some of the details

call to mind the style of dress preferred by her daughter for her favourite heroines'.

Maria's Aunt Jane had married John Fennell, the recently appointed headmaster of the Wesleyan Methodist boarding school at Woodhouse Grove, near Leeds. Aunt Jane was to take charge of the school's domestic arrangements and Maria came to assist her. In July Patrick Brontë was invited to examine the boys at Woodhouse Grove in the classics, having known John Fennell in Wellington, where he had also met the Reverend William Morgan, who was engaged to the Fennells' daughter, Jane. By the end of August Maria had agreed to marry Mr Brontë. It appears to have been a love match. A few weeks before the marriage, Maria wrote to him:

Surely after this you can have no doubt that you possess all my heart. Two months ago I could not possibly have believed that you would ever engross so much of my thoughts and affections, and far less could I have thought that I should be so forward as to tell you so … I feel that my heart is more ready to attach itself to earth than heaven.

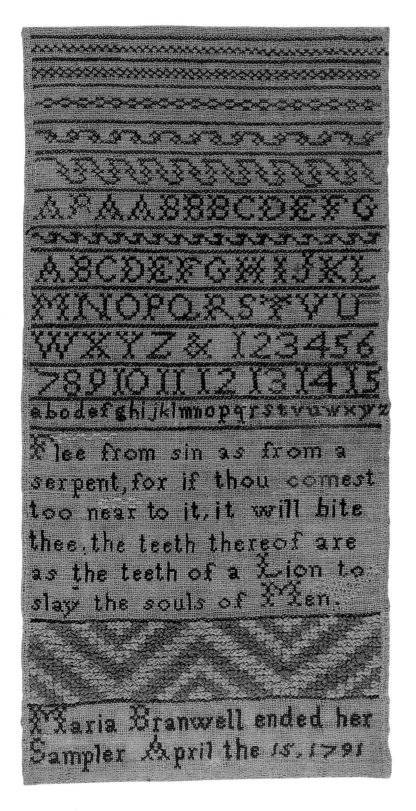

When Patrick and Maria were married on 29 December 1812 at St Oswald's Church at Guiseley, Maria's cousin Jane married William Morgan at the same time, the two grooms each performing the marriage service for the other couple and the brides acting as each other's bridesmaid. On the same day at Madron Church in Penzance, Maria's youngest sister Charlotte was married to her cousin, Joseph Branwell.

The couple probably began married life at Lousy Thorn Farm, where Patrick had lodged before his marriage. They then moved to Clough House at Hightown, where their two eldest children, Maria and Elizabeth, were born. In 1815 the Brontë family moved to Thornton, near Bradford, where Maria gave birth to four more children.

Maria has been described as something of a blue-stocking, and while at Thornton she wrote an essay entitled 'The Advantages of Poverty in Religious Concerns'. After her death, Patrick Brontë added a footnote to the manuscript: 'The above was written by my dear Wife, and sent for insertion in one of the periodical publications – Keep it, as a memorial of her.' In the essay Maria argues that poverty is not an evil in itself because the poor are more able to live a religious life, not being distracted by the diversions of wealth. Although her arguments may seem naïve today, she wrote with great sincerity and was representing views that would have been quite widespread in Evangelical religious thinking of the time. Perhaps the greatest significance of this manuscript is the example it set for her daughters of a woman writing with a view to publication.

A sampler worked by the Brontës' mother when she was a young girl.

Despite Maria's continual pregnancies, the family enjoyed a pleasant social life at Thornton, centred on the wealthy Firth family at Kipping House and their wide circle of friends. This changed in 1820 when the family made their final move to Haworth, for Maria was taken ill shortly after with what is believed to have been uterine cancer. While her children played quietly in another part of the house, Maria was confined to her bedroom, enduring months of agonizing pain. Her nurse, Martha Wright, remembered how on her better days, Maria would ask to be raised in bed so that she could watch her cleaning the grate, 'because she did it as it was done in Cornwall'. Martha also heard Maria crying out in anguish, 'Oh God my poor children – Oh God my poor children!' All the servants remembered Maria's distress at the sight of her soon-to-be-motherless children, and how she could only bear to see them one at a time. When she died on 15 September 1821, her husband and sister were at her bedside, and her children, with their nurse, were at the foot of the bed. Her mind was 'often disturbed' in the last conflict, wrote Patrick Brontë, adding that she died, 'if not triumphantly, at least calmly and with a holy yet humble confidence that Christ was her Saviour and heaven her eternal home'.

ABOVE *A watercolour painting of 25 Chapel Street, Penzance, home of Maria and Elizabeth Branwell.*

OPPOSITE *It is believed that Patrick Brontë proposed to Maria Branwell in the romantic ruins of Kirkstall Abbey, near Leeds.*

Mr Brontë preserved the series of letters Maria had written to him during their courtship, and long after Maria's death, he gave Charlotte some of her mother's letters to read, an experience she found deeply moving:

Papa put into my hands a little packet of letters and papers – telling me that they were Mama's and that I might read them – I did read them in a frame of mind I cannot describe – the papers were yellow with time all having been written before I was born – it was strange to peruse now for the first time the records of a mind whence my own sprang – and most strange – and at once sad and sweet to find that mind of a truly fine, pure and elevated order … I wished She had lived and that I had known her.

LEFT *The fireplace in the old Parsonage at Thornton, in the room where Charlotte, Branwell, Emily and Anne were born.*

ABOVE *In April 1820 the Brontës moved from Thornton to Haworth and made their slow ascent of the steep Main Street, with all their possessions loaded on to horse-drawn carts.*

RIGHT *Charlotte Brontë's copy of a portrait of Mrs Brontë, painted in October 1830 when Charlotte was fourteen years old.*

ELIZABETH BRANWELL

*Miss Branwell, arrived, and afforded great comfort to my mind,
which has been the case ever since, by sharing my labours and sorrows,
and behaving as an affectionate mother to my children.*

PATRICK BRONTË, letter to the Reverend John Buckworth, 1821

Miss Branwell was, I believe, [wrote Mrs Gaskell in *The Life of Charlotte Brontë*] a kindly and conscientious woman, with a good deal of character, but with the somewhat narrow ideas natural to one who had spent nearly all her life in the same place. She had strong prejudices, and soon took a distaste to Yorkshire … The children respected her, and had that sort of affection for her which is generated by esteem; but I do not think they ever freely loved her.

Elizabeth Branwell had spent over a year with the Brontë family at Thornton, before in 1821 at the age of forty-five, she left her comfortable home in Penzance to care for her sister's six young children. She must have felt serious

Haworth churchyard in snow. Having come from the soft, warm climate of Penzance, Elizabeth Branwell dreaded the cold and damp of Yorkshire, and rarely left the house, except to go to church. As Mrs Gaskell wrote in THE LIFE OF CHARLOTTE BRONTË: 'it was a great change for a lady considerably past forty to come and take up her abode in a place … where the snow lay long and late on the moors, stretching bleakly and barely up from the dwelling which was henceforward to be her home.'

misgivings at the idea of making her home with them on a permanent basis. She never saw Cornwall again and died at Haworth in 1842.

At Haworth Miss Branwell took possession of the room that had formerly been her sister's, and here she taught her young nieces sewing and the essential arts of household management. Haworth must have seemed like an alien world, and she rarely set a foot outside the Parsonage except to go to church. Being used to the gentle climate of Cornwall, she could not stand the cold and kept a fire burning constantly in her bedroom grate. She is remembered for clicking around the house in wooden overshoes, known as pattens, to protect her feet from the damp flagstone floors of the Parsonage.

Recalling her first visit to the Parsonage in 1833, Charlotte's school friend Ellen Nussey described Miss Branwell as 'a very small antiquated little lady, she wore caps large enough for half a dozen of the present fashion, and a front of light auburn curls over her forehead … she always dressed in silk. The social life of her younger days she appeared to recall with regret.'

Aunt Branwell has often been portrayed in biographies as an embittered spinster and a repressive influence on the Brontë children. In her biography of Anne Brontë, Winifred Gerin goes so far as to claim that 'sad as their motherless childhood must have been it need never have been "oppressed with sin and woe" but for the gloomy regimen of the maiden Aunt.' There is no real evidence to support such accusations, for Miss Branwell was, like her sister, a lively, intelligent woman who saved for her nieces' futures and provided companionship for Mr Brontë. His eyesight was poor, and she would spend a portion of every day reading aloud to him. Ellen Nussey recalled how discussions on what they had been reading would continue at the tea table, and how Miss Branwell 'tilted argument without fear against Mr Brontë'. She had been considered a 'belle' among her circle in Cornwall, and liked to shock guests by offering them a pinch of her snuff.

Miss Branwell died in October 1842 aged sixty-six and was buried in the vault beneath the floor of Haworth Church. In a letter written shortly after her death, Branwell Brontë described her as 'the guide and director of all the happy days connected with my childhood'. Although the Brontë children may not have 'freely loved her', they certainly 'respected her', for she brought order and stability into their lives. She was financially independent, and for twenty-one years contributed to household expenses. She also, indirectly, enabled the Brontë sisters to become authors, for without their inheritance from Aunt Branwell, they would not have been able to pay for the publication of *Poems* in 1846 and *Wuthering Heights* and *Agnes Grey* in 1847.

MARIA AND ELIZABETH BRONTË

She would talk much of her two dead sisters, Maria and Elizabeth.
Her love for them was most intense; a kind of adoration dwelt in her feelings
which, as she conversed, almost imparted itself to her listener.

ELLEN NUSSEY'S REMINISCENCES, 1871

We know very little about Maria and Elizabeth, the two eldest Brontë sisters, who died within a few weeks of each other in 1825. There are no surviving portraits of the two girls and we do not know the exact date of Maria's birth. Maria was baptized at Hartshead Church on 23 April 1814. Elizabeth was born on 8 February 1815, shortly before the family moved to Thornton, where she was baptized on 26 August.

During Mrs Brontë's illness, seven-year-old Maria took charge of her younger brother and sisters. 'You would not have known there was a child in the house,' their mother's nurse told Mrs Gaskell; 'they were such still, noiseless, good little creatures.' The children would walk out on the moors or Maria would read the newspapers aloud to them. Mr Brontë told Mrs Gaskell that Maria 'had a powerfully intellectual mind', and that long before her death, he was able to discuss with her 'any of the leading topics of the day with as much freedom and pleasure as with any grown-up person'.

When the time came to send his eldest daughters to school, Elizabeth Firth, a family friend from Thornton, suggested her own old school, Crofton Hall, near Wakefield.

Maria and Elizabeth went there in 1823, but the fees were expensive and their stay was brief. When a new school for the daughters of impoverished clergymen was opened at Cowan Bridge, near Kirkby Lonsdale, it must have seemed like an ideal solution. The cost of board and education was heavily subsidized by an impressive list of patrons, which meant that Patrick could afford to send all his daughters to school.

On 21 July 1824, Maria and Elizabeth arrived at Cowan Bridge, to be followed by Charlotte in August and Emily in November. The school registers show that the Brontë sisters, with the exception of Elizabeth, were to receive the higher level of education that would equip them to become governesses. Possibly Elizabeth had been selected to become the family housekeeper, making the extra accomplishments unnecessary in her case.

This first experience of formal schooling had disastrous consequences for the entire family. The school regime was harsh; Charlotte's descriptions in *Jane Eyre* of the grim Lowood School were drawn from her experiences at Cowan Bridge. In her biography of Charlotte, Mrs Gaskell claimed that 'Miss Brontë more than once said to me, that she should

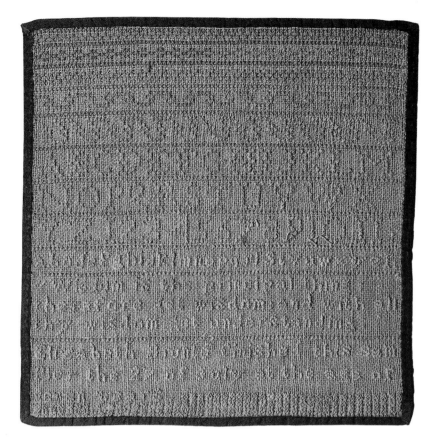

not have written what she did of Lowood in *Jane Eyre*, if she thought the place would have been so immediately identified with Cowan Bridge, although there was not a word in her account of the institution but what was true at the time when she knew it.'

Former pupils who were at Cowan Bridge at the same time as the Brontës remembered how Maria was persecuted by an underteacher at the school, and how she bore her punishments with stoicism. Maria was immortalized as the

ABOVE *These faded samplers are the only surviving relics of the two eldest Brontë children. Maria's sampler was completed on 18 May when she was eight years old, and Elizabeth's on 22 July when she was seven.*

saintly Helen Burns in *Jane Eyre*, but Elizabeth seems to have left little impression on her fellow pupils. One of the few surviving accounts of Elizabeth comes from the superintendent at Cowan Bridge and relates to a mysterious accident she suffered there:

The second, Elizabeth, is the only one of the family of whom I have a vivid recollection, from her meeting with a somewhat alarming accident, in consequence of which I had her for some days and nights in my bed-room, not only for the sake of her greater quiet, but that I might watch over her myself. Her head was severely cut, but she bore all the consequent suffering with exemplary patience, and by it won much upon my esteem.

Towards the close of winter, an epidemic of 'low fever' or typhus broke out in the school and many pupils became ill. Maria also became ill, but with tuberculosis rather than typhus. Mr Brontë was summoned, and he fetched his daughter home on 14 February 1825. Maria died at the Parsonage on 6 May, aged eleven. She was buried in the vault beneath the church floor, next to her mother. Elizabeth was also showing signs of consumption, and the news of Maria's death prompted the school authorities to send her home. Patrick was so shocked by her condition that he withdrew Charlotte and

LEFT *Every Sunday the pupils from the Clergy Daughters' School had to walk a distance of over two miles across fields to attend Tunstall Church. It would have been a pleasant walk on a fine day, but in winter the girls would often arrive cold and wet and sit shivering through the service.*

OPPOSITE ABOVE *The Clergy Daughters' School at Cowan Bridge, from an engraving of 1824. The school was immortalized as the infamous Lowood School in Charlotte's novel* JANE EYRE.

OPPOSITE BELOW THE CHILD'S FIRST TALES *was produced by the Reverend William Carus Wilson, founder of the Clergy Daughters' School at Cowan Bridge, and was in regular use at the school. The text reveals a preoccupation with infant mortality, often accompanied by gruesome woodcut illustrations of punishment and death.*

MARIA AND ELIZABETH BRONTË

Emily from the school. They arrived back home in time to witness Elizabeth's death on 15 June, aged ten.

The girls' early deaths must have been devastating for the family, especially as Maria, and to a lesser extent Elizabeth, had taken on the role of mother to their younger brother and sisters. Charlotte was haunted for the rest of her life by the experience of helplessly watching her sisters suffer, and motherless children became a feature of the Brontës' writings. Reminiscing many years later, Ellen Nussey recalled how Charlotte would often talk about her dead sisters:

> She described Maria as a little mother among the rest, superhuman in goodness and cleverness. But most touching of all were the revelations of her sufferings, – how she suffered with the sensibility of a grown-up person, and endured with a patience and fortitude that were Christ-like. Charlotte would still weep and suffer when thinking of her. She talked of Elizabeth also, but never with the anguish of expression which accompanied her recollections of Maria.

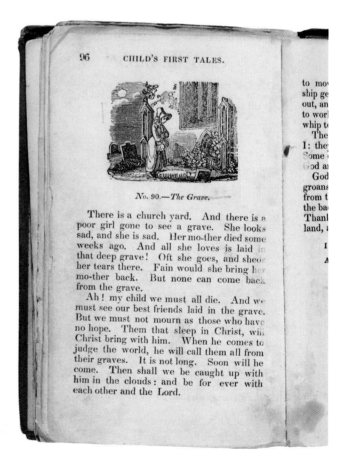

CHARLOTTE BRONTË

Lewes was describing Currer Bell to me yesterday, as a little, plain, provincial, sickly looking old maid. Yet what passion, what fire in her!

GEORGE ELIOT, letter, 1853

The deaths of Maria and Elizabeth Brontë in 1825 meant that the responsibilities of an eldest child fell to nine-year-old Charlotte Brontë. Many years later, Charlotte's friend and biographer Elizabeth Gaskell wrote: 'I can well imagine that the grave serious composure, which, when I knew her, gave her face the dignity of an old Venetian portrait, was no acquisition of later years, but dated from that early age when she found herself in the position of an elder sister to motherless children.'

For the next few years the surviving four children remained at the Parsonage, receiving lessons from their father and creating a rich imaginary world. It seems significant that, having recently lost their much-loved elder sisters, the children imaginatively transformed themselves into genii, with the power to mete out terrible punishments and to bring the dead back to life. The children chronicled the events taking place in their fantasy world in tiny books, and Charlotte joined forces with Branwell in a literary partnership that was to be of crucial importance in the development of her later writing.

Charlotte understood from an early age that her father's lack of a private income meant that she and her sisters would one day have to earn their own livings. The only socially acceptable career option available to impoverished middle-class women was teaching – either in a school or privately as a governess in a family. With this end in view,

FAR LEFT *A view from Penistone Hill along the edge of Sladen Valley out on to the moors. Charlotte and her sisters would follow this route to the waterfall and the higher ground beyond.*

ABOVE *This hand-sown little book is the earliest known manuscript by Charlotte, written at the age of twelve. The story opens with the line 'There was once a little girl and her name was Ane' and was intended for her little sister. The book is illustrated by six tiny watercolour vignettes and a map of the Brontës' imaginary world, Glasstown.*

BELOW LEFT *Roe Head, Miss Wooler's School at Mirfield, where Charlotte met her lifelong friends Ellen Nussey and Mary Taylor.*

in January 1831 at the age of fourteen Charlotte was sent to Miss Wooler's school at Roe Head to acquire the accomplishments that would qualify her to teach. One of the earliest descriptions we have of her dates from this time, written by another pupil, Mary Taylor:

> I first saw her coming out of a covered cart, in very old-fashioned clothes, and looking very cold and miserable. She was coming to school at Miss Wooler's. When she appeared in the schoolroom, her dress was changed, but just as old. She looked a little old woman, so short-sighted that she always appeared to be seeking something, and moving her head from side to side to catch a sight of it. She was very shy and nervous, and spoke with a strong Irish accent.

The small community of pupils at Roe Head consisted of the daughters of local manufacturers. Mary and Ellen Nussey, who became Charlotte's friends, were both fashionably dressed, attractive girls. Charlotte, always painfully conscious of her plainness, felt herself marked out as an oddity. When it came to her intellectual abilities, however, she was far more confident. She was a voracious reader and had read many of the popular books of the period as well as her father's classical texts. Not surprisingly for a clergyman's daughter, she knew the Bible inside out; and she was almost equally familiar with the works of Lord Byron – usually deemed unsuitable reading for young ladies. Only a few months before leaving for Roe Head, Charlotte had compiled a 'Catalogue' of books she had written, listing twenty-two volumes in total. It must have been a great mortification to find herself placed in the second class. 'We thought her very ignorant,' Mary recalled, 'for she had never learnt grammar at all, and very little geography.' But Charlotte's knowledge of art and literature more than made up for her lack of formal education. Mary remembered how Charlotte

would confound us by knowing things that were out of our range altogether. She was acquainted with most of the short pieces of poetry that we had to learn by heart; would tell us the authors, the poems they were taken from, and sometimes repeat a page or two, and tell us the plot ... She used to draw much better, and more quickly, than anything we had seen before, and knew much about celebrated pictures and painters . . . She made poetry and drawing, at least exceedingly interesting to me.

ABOVE *A recently discovered chalk portrait of Charlotte Brontë by an unknown artist.*

OPPOSITE *Charlotte was acutely aware of what she regarded as her plain appearance and caricatured herself in this illustrated letter from Brussels as an ugly dwarf (she was approximately four feet ten inches tall). However, in later years she rejected the cult of the beautiful heroine and followed the precedent of her sister Anne in creating a plain protagonist in* JANE EYRE.

Charlotte worked hard and flourished at Roe Head, not only rising to the top of the first class but also taking away a silver medal for achievement. On her return to the Parsonage, she passed on the education she had received to her sisters, later returning to Roe Head as a teacher. Over the next few years she spent brief and unhappy periods working as a governess.

To escape the hated life of the governess, the sisters decided to set up a school of their own at the Parsonage, which would at least enable them to stay together. In order to acquire the language skills that would attract pupils and ensure the school's success, Charlotte decided that she and Emily should spend time at a school on the continent. In February 1842, supported by their aunt's money, Charlotte and Emily travelled to Brussels to study at the Pensionnat Heger, a well-respected girls' day school that also took some boarding pupils. The reason Charlotte gave her Aunt Branwell for wishing to go abroad was that if they were to start a school in Haworth, improving their languages in Brussels would give them a competitive advantage. The full truth seems to be that Charlotte, tempted by descriptions of Brussels in the letters of the Taylor sisters, who were already studying there, longed to spread her wings. Aunt Branwell's money would support the sisters for only six months, but Charlotte envisaged that she and Emily would teach to earn enough to stay for at least a year. They remained until October, when they were recalled by news from home of their aunt's illness and impending death. They arrived too late for her funeral. When the sisters returned to Haworth, they carried with them a letter from Monsieur Heger to their father in which he expressed his regret at losing such exceptional pupils. He stressed how, given 'another year at the most', their studies would have been 'completed and well completed'.

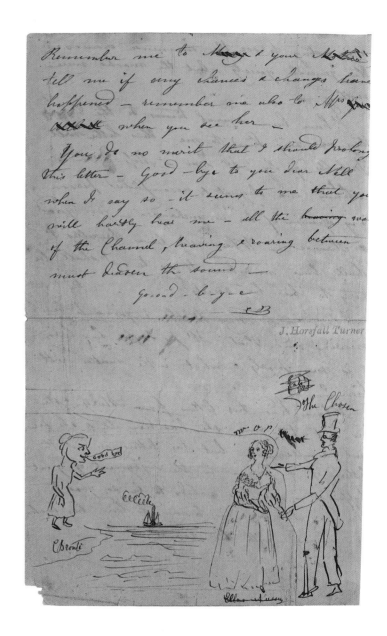

Both sisters were committed to reading and learning, but while Emily was content to remain at Haworth, Heger's letter provided a strong inducement for Charlotte to return to Brussels, alone, the following year. She remained at the Pensionnat until January 1844, although she gradually became low in spirits and homesick. Following her return to Haworth the school project came to nothing. A prospectus

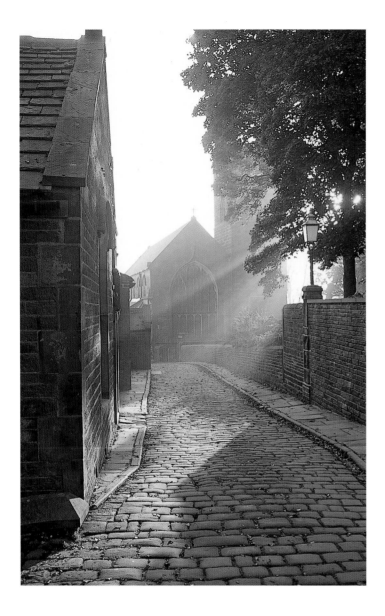

world. Although she did not completely succeed, she began to make use of her own experience in her writing. The schools and private houses where she had taught would eventually provide the subject matter and settings for her novels.

In 1846 the three sisters – Charlotte, Emily and Anne – financed the publication of a collection of their poems, using the pseudonyms Currer, Ellis and Acton Bell. Despite the fact that only two copies of the book were sold, the sisters' appetite for publication had been whetted, and negotiating arrangements with the printers provided a much-needed focus for Charlotte's energies following the failure of the school project. It was not long before three prose tales by the Bells were making their way round the London publishing houses. Charlotte's tale, *The Professor*, was rejected several times before it arrived at the offices of Smith, Elder & Co. Although it was rejected once again, the firm's reader, William Smith Williams, recognized the author's potential and expressed an interest in any future work. Charlotte was already at work on *Jane Eyre*, which the firm published in 1847.

What began as a formal business correspondence with her publishers developed into a friendship. In her letters to Williams, Charlotte discussed the books she had been reading and shared her sense of loss following the deaths of Branwell, Emily and Anne, which all occurred within two years of the publication of *Jane Eyre*. Charlotte turned to her writing as a refuge through the dark days ahead, and took up her novel *Shirley* once more. This was published in October 1849, and as the first anniversary of Emily's death approached, Charlotte fled Haworth to stay with her publisher George Smith and his family in London.

Over the next few years Charlotte made several visits to London, and as her true identity gradually became known,

was printed and circulated but not a single pupil could be found. By this time Charlotte did not very much care, for she was suffering the pain of unrequited passion for her married teacher, Monsieur Heger – the only man outside her family circle to take her writing ambitions seriously.

The sisters had continued to write since childhood, and following her return from Brussels, Charlotte made a conscious decision to tear herself away from her fantasy

CHARLOTTE BRONTË

her fame brought her a great deal of attention – some of it welcome, some of it not. In 1850 she accepted an invitation to visit Sir James Kay-Shuttleworth and his wife at their summer residence above Lake Windermere, where she met the novelist Elizabeth Gaskell.

Ellen Nussey believed that Charlotte's publisher discussed marriage with her friend, a suggestion that Charlotte denied, claiming that she was 'content to have him as a friend – and pray God to continue to me the commonsense to look on one so young, so rising and so hopeful in no other light.' When Charlotte submitted the third volume of the manuscript of *Villette* to her publisher, there was an unusual silence from Smith. This may have been due to his uncomfortable recognition of himself in the portrayal of Dr John in the novel. Their correspondence never recovered its former warmth, and relations cooled still further after Smith announced his engagement to Elizabeth Blakeway, the beautiful daughter of a London wine merchant.

Charlotte herself had recently rejected a marriage proposal from her father's curate, the Reverend Arthur Bell Nicholls. Patrick Brontë was incensed at the thought of the poor Irish curate proposing marriage to his famous daughter and treated him with harshness and contempt, but her father's unjust treatment worked in Nicholls' favour, and the couple were married in Haworth Church on 29 June 1854. Despite Charlotte's misgivings, the marriage was happy, although short-lived.

OPPOSITE *A view of Church Street with the Sunday school on the left. Charlotte and Mr Nicholls entertained the Sunday school teachers and scholars to supper here after their marriage in 1854.*

RIGHT *A carte-de-visite photograph of Arthur Bell Nicholls.*

Charlotte died on the morning of 31 March 1855. She is believed to have been in the early stages of pregnancy. The Reverend Sutcliffe Sowden, who had officiated at her wedding just nine months earlier, was recalled to Haworth to conduct her funeral service. In 1857, two years after Charlotte's death, her first novel, *The Professor*, was finally published, along with Elizabeth Gaskell's moving tribute to her friend, *The Life of Charlotte Brontë*.

BRANWELL BRONTË

He was very clever, no doubt; perhaps, to begin with, the greatest genius in this rare family. The sisters hardly recognised their own, or each others' powers, but they knew his.

ELIZABETH GASKELL, *The Life of Charlotte Brontë*, 1857

Patrick Branwell Brontë, the fourth Brontë child, was educated at home by his father and, like his sisters, he read widely from an early age. The loss of his two elder sisters shortly before his eighth birthday in 1825 was an event from which he never fully recovered.

Over the next few years, Branwell and his remaining sisters began to make up and act out plays. Charlotte and Branwell took the lead in inventing an imaginary kingdom, inspired by descriptions of the interior of Africa in the family's well-thumbed copy of Goldsmith's *Grammar of General Geography*. The chief city was Glasstown, later Verdopolis, and eventually in 1834 the kingdom of Angria was created.

Although all the Brontës possessed intellectual and artistic ability, Patrick occupied the privileged position of the only boy in the family. Although Mr Brontë chose to educate his son at home rather than sending him away to school, and later rejected university on the grounds that it would 'require great expense, and four or five years from hence, ere he could, in a pecuniary way, do any thing for himself', education had played an important role in Mr Brontë's life and, as Branwell would be starting out on his career from a much more advantageous situation in life, his family, not surprisingly, expected great things of him. When Branwell showed talent for drawing and painting, he was given lessons in oils, the medium of professional artists, with

the distinguished Leeds artist William Robinson. It was during this period that Branwell completed the well-known portrait of his sisters. He originally included himself in the composition, but painted himself out in what turned out to be a strangely prophetic act. It was hoped that Branwell would enter the Royal Academy of Arts, but the idea never seems to have progressed beyond the planning stage, becoming instead the first in a series of disappointments and failures that marred Branwell's life.

Branwell's artistic career began and ended in Bradford, where he set up as a portrait painter in 1838. Competing with the area's well-established artists must have been discouraging, and Branwell found it preferable to join the lively company of young artists and writers who met in the George Hotel. The news that his teacher, William Robinson, had died destitute despite his status as a Royal Academician cannot have held out much encouragement to Branwell, and he returned home in debt within a year.

LEFT *A watercolour painting by Branwell, entitled* PRAISE *and dated 9 September 1830. It is a copy from a print of a painting by Raphael depicting St Cecilia, the patron saint of music and musicians. She is pictured with her particular attribute, the organ, and makes a fitting subject for Branwell, who was extremely musical and played the flute, piano and church organ.*

RIGHT *A caricature self-portrait of Branwell Brontë,* c.1840.

He always hoped to carve out a career in literature, and wrote several times offering his services and sending samples of his poetry to *Blackwood's Edinburgh Magazine*, the Brontës' favourite childhood reading. His arrogant enthusiasm ensured that his letters remained unanswered. In 1840 he became tutor to the sons of Mr Postlethwaite at Broughton-in-Furness. In a letter he wrote to John Brown, the sexton, intended to impress his Haworth friends, Branwell described a night of riotous drinking at the Kendal Hotel, en route to his new employment. For a time, proximity to the Lake District and its rich associations with the Romantic poets inspired Branwell. He sent samples of his work to Hartley Coleridge, who expressed admiration for his translations of Horace's *Odes* and invited Branwell to visit his home at Grasmere. Within six months Branwell was dismissed from his post, allegedly for drinking.

Two months later Branwell was employed as assistant clerk at Sowerby Bridge on the new Leeds–Manchester railway, before being promoted to clerk-in-charge at Luddenden Foot, where he was once again dismissed, this time for negligence in keeping the accounts. Francis Leyland, brother of Branwell's sculptor friend Joseph, left a description of Branwell dating from this time:

In person he was rather below the middle height, but of a refined and gentleman-like appearance, and of graceful manners. His complexion was fair and his features handsome; his mouth and chin were well-shaped; his nose was prominent and of the Roman type; his eyes sparkled and danced with delight, and his forehead made up a face of oval form which gave an irresistible charm to its possessor, and attracted the admiration of those who knew him.

LEFT *Grasmere, the Lakeland home of William Wordsworth, which Branwell visited when he worked as a tutor at Broughton-in-Furness and was invited to the home of Hartley Coleridge, who lived near by.*

RIGHT *The Lord Nelson inn at Luddenden, one of Branwell's haunts when working on the railway.*

Not everyone was so kind. Francis Grundy, a young engineer who met Branwell at this time, described him as 'almost insignificantly small', with 'a mass of red hair, which he wore brushed high off his forehead, – to help his height, I fancy … small ferrety eyes, deep sunk, and still further hidden by the never removed spectacles'.

In the 1840s Branwell achieved a measure of success when several of his poems appeared in local newspapers, making him the first of the Brontë siblings to become a published poet. Although Branwell had abandoned the imaginary world he created in childhood, his poems were published under the pseudonym Northangerland, the name

of his Angrian alter ego, suggesting that the fantasy world still retained a hold. He increasingly found the demands of everyday life difficult to cope with and, with a string of humiliating failures behind him, was fast becoming a cause for concern.

In 1843, while Anne Brontë was working as governess to the Robinson family of Thorp Green Hall, near York, it was arranged that Branwell would join her there as tutor to the Robinsons' only son. Two years later Anne left her post, followed shortly afterwards by Branwell, who was dismissed in disgrace for 'proceedings bad beyond expression' – allegedly a love affair with Lydia Robinson, the wife of his

OPPOSITE *The Monk's House at Thorp Green, where Branwell lodged when tutor to Edmund Robinson.*

RIGHT *A PARODY, Branwell Brontë's last known drawing, made two months before his death in 1848 and showing himself being summoned from sleep by Death.*

employer. After the death of her husband, when it became clear that Mrs Robinson had no intention of marrying him, Branwell turned to alcohol and opium, causing his family much embarrassment and distress.

Branwell had begun work on a novel, which was never completed. It is not known for sure whether he was aware of his sisters' literary achievements when he died suddenly on 24 September 1848, at the age of thirty-one, repenting the fact that in all his life he had 'done nothing either great or good'. Charlotte, his closest companion in childhood, could not forgive her brother's inability to fulfil his early promise. Shortly after his death she wrote:

Branwell was his Father's and his sisters' pride and hope in boyhood, but since Manhood, the case has been otherwise … I do not weep from a sense of bereavement – there is no prop withdrawn, no consolation torn away, no dear companion lost – but for the wreck of talent, the ruin of promise, the untimely dreary extinction of what might have been a burning and a shining light. My brother was my junior; I had aspirations and ambitions for him once – long ago – they have perished mournfully – nothing remains of him but a memory of errors and sufferings – There is such a bitterness of pity for his life and death – such a yearning for the emptiness of his whole existence as I cannot describe.

EMILY BRONTË

In Emily's nature the extremes of vigour and simplicity seemed to meet. Under an unsophisticated culture, inartificial tastes, and an unpretending outside, lay a secret power and fire that might have informed the brain and kindled the veins of a hero.

CHARLOTTE BRONTË, *Biographical Notice of Ellis and Acton Bell*, 1850

Born on 30 July 1818 at the Parsonage at Thornton, Emily Jane Brontë was baptized on 20 August in the Old Bell Chapel, where her father officiated as Perpetual Curate. Before Emily's second birthday the family moved to the Parsonage at Haworth, and the moorland setting came to have a profound influence on Emily's writing.

Following the death of her mother in 1821, Emily and her sisters learnt the essential female skills of needlework and household management from their Aunt Branwell, who taught the girls their letters and a smattering of French. They studied the Bible with their father, and were allowed to share their brother's more academic lessons in history and geography.

In 1824 Emily experienced her first taste of formal schooling, when she was sent, along with her elder sisters, to the Clergy Daughters' School at Cowan Bridge, near Kirkby Lonsdale – an experience that ended tragically with the deaths of Maria and Elizabeth. While Charlotte never forgot the hardships the sisters suffered at the school, the experience seems to have left Emily relatively unscathed.

When the surviving children resumed their lessons at the Parsonage with their father and aunt, Emily and Anne began

to resent the dominance of Charlotte and Branwell in the creation of the plays the children began to write and act out at this time. Some time around 1833 they formed an alliance of their own and developed the world of Gondal. We know that Emily and Anne produced many books relating to the Gondal saga and that their world was probably as complex as Angria; however, none of the prose works has survived.

When Ellen Nussey visited the Parsonage at this time, she noted that Emily had now

> acquired a lithesome graceful figure. She was the tallest person in the house except her Father, her hair which was naturally as beautiful as Charlotte's was in the same unbecoming tight curl and frizz, and there was the same want of complexion. She had very beautiful eyes, kind, kindling, liquid eyes, sometimes they looked grey, sometimes dark blue but she did not often look at you, she was too reserved. She talked very little, she and Anne were like twins, inseperable companions, and in the very closest sympathy which never had any interruption.

In 1835 Emily was sent to Miss Wooler's school at Roe Head, Mirfield, where Charlotte was employed as a teacher. At seventeen, she was probably the oldest pupil there,

a reserved, awkward girl who did not make friends. Many years later, in a prefatory note that accompanied a selection of Emily's poems, Charlotte described how her sister was unable to cope with school life:

The change from her own home to a school, and from her own very noiseless, very secluded, but unrestricted and inartificial mode of life, to one of disciplined routine (though under the kindliest auspices), was what she failed in enduring … Every morning when she woke, the vision of home and the moors rushed on her, and darkened and saddened the day that lay before her. In this struggle her health was quickly broken … I felt in my heart she would die if she did not go home, and with this conviction obtained her recall.

Within three months Emily was back at home in Haworth. Anne, who proved more adaptable, was dispatched to Roe Head in her place. Emily had established her right to remain at home, and only ever made one attempt to earn her living. That was in 1838, when, despite her lack of formal education, she obtained a post at Miss Patchett's school at Law Hill, near Halifax. In a letter to Ellen Nussey, Charlotte commented:

> My sister Emily is gone into a situation as a teacher in a large school of near forty pupils near Halifax. I have had one letter from her since her departure it gives an appalling account of her duties – Hard labour from six in the morning until near eleven at night with only one half hour of exercise between – this is slavery I fear she will never stand it.

Emily did not stand it for long. The demands of teaching left her little time to indulge in her Gondal fantasies, and a few months later, after reputedly informing her pupils that she much preferred the school's dog to any of them, Emily was back at Haworth once again. When the sisters decided to set up a school of their own at the Parsonage and Charlotte decided that she should spend time at a school on the continent, it seems surprising that she chose Emily to accompany her, and more surprising still that Emily agreed to go.

At the Pensionnat Heger in Brussels, Monsieur Heger soon became aware of the Brontës' outstanding abilities. Charlotte reported that he and Emily did not 'draw well together at all', although according to Mrs Gaskell, he 'seems to have rated Emily's genius as something even higher than Charlotte's'. Heger believed Emily had 'a head for logic, and a capability of argument, unusual in a man, and rare indeed in a woman', and this capacity soon made itself felt. After an initial assessment of his new pupils, Heger devised a different teaching approach. He proposed to read them works by some of the greatest French writers, to analyse certain passages and then set them to produce a piece of their own, 'catching the echo' of another author's style. In *The Life of Charlotte Brontë*, Mrs Gaskell describes their reaction, after Monsieur Heger had explained his plan: 'Emily spoke first; and said she saw no good to be derived from it; and that, by adopting it, they should lose all originality of thought and expression. She would have entered into an argument on the subject, but for this, M. Heger had no time.'

FAR LEFT *A diary paper, dated 24 November 1834, written jointly by Emily and Anne. As well as providing glimpses of parsonage life, the paper expresses the sisters' hopes for the future, which has a particular poignancy when we read it today: 'Anne and I say I wonder what we shall be like and what we shall be if all goes well in the year 1874 – in which year I shall be in my 57th year Anne will be going in her 55th year Branwell will be going in his 58th year And Charlotte in her 59th year hoping we shall all be well at that time We close our paper.'*

LEFT *Law Hill, near Halifax, scene of Emily's brief, unhappy spell as a teacher.*

RIGHT *A tree-lined path leading from the village to the moors, reminiscent of Emily's poem 'A little and a lone green lane'.*

Despite the restrictions imposed upon them, both sisters managed to produce essays that remained distinctively original. Heger's lessons were fundamental to Charlotte's emergence as a great writer, but his long-term influence on Emily is more difficult to assess.

After the sisters' stay in Brussels was cut short by the news of Aunt Branwell's illness and death, Emily remained at the Parsonage as housekeeper, while Charlotte returned to Brussels for another year. When the school project foundered, in her diary paper (Emily and Anne wrote diary papers at intervals of approximately four years, when the previous papers would be opened and read) for July 1845 Emily wrote:

> I should have mentioned that last summer the school scheme was revived in full vigour – we had prospectuses printed despatched letters to all acquaintances imparting our plans and did our little all – but it was found no go – now I don't desire a school at all and none of us have any great longing for it – we have cash enough for our present wants with a prospect of accumulation.

The 'cash' that Emily mentions is a reference to the shares in the York and North Midland Railway the sisters inherited on Aunt Branwell's death. In all, they inherited just under three hundred pounds each – not a huge amount, but enough to give a sense of security. Emily threw herself into the old routine of household chores combined with writing. It was during this period that she wrote some of her most powerful and haunting poems.

When Charlotte discovered Emily's poems, she was struck by their quality and, suspecting that a mind like Emily's 'could not be without some latent spark of honourable ambition', she hatched a plan to publish a selection of poems by all three sisters. Charlotte's assessment appears to have been correct and Emily eventually agreed to the publication of her poems. When the volume failed to sell, she set to work on a novel, written with a view to publication. When the novel, *Wuthering Heights*, failed to find a publisher, she was prepared to pay to see it in print.

Within a year of the publication of *Wuthering Heights*, Emily was dead. It is said that Emily caught cold at Branwell's funeral in 1848 and never left the house again. She refused to be reliant on others when she was ill. Charlotte found her sister's self-sufficient attitude baffling, writing less than two months before Emily's death:

> I would fain hope that Emily is a little better this evening, but it is difficult to ascertain this: she is a real stoic in illness, she neither seeks nor will accept sympathy … you must look on, and see her do what she is unfit to do, and not dare to say a word … When she is ill there seems to be no sunshine in the world for me; the tie of sister is near and dear indeed, and I think a certain harshness in her powerful, and peculiar character only makes me cling to her more.

Emily refused medical assistance and died from tuberculosis on 19 December 1848 at the age of thirty. It is thought that she may have been working on a second novel at the time of her death, although a manuscript has never come to light.

ANNE BRONTË

Anne's character was milder and more subdued; she wanted the power, the fire,
the originality of her sister, but was well-endowed with quiet virtues of her own.
Long-suffering, self-denying, reflective, and intelligent, a constitutional reserve
and taciturnity placed and kept her in the shade, and covered her mind, and especially
her feelings, with a sort of nun-like veil, which was rarely lifted.

CHARLOTTE BRONTË, *Biographical Notice of Ellis and Acton Bell*, 1850

Anne Brontë, the youngest member of the Brontë family, is usually seen as having lived her life in the shadow of her elder sisters. Much of what we know of Anne comes from Charlotte, who always regarded Anne as the baby of the family. Mrs Gaskell described Anne as 'that gentle little one' – a perception she picked up from Charlotte, despite the fact that Anne had written a powerful realistic novel that critics condemned for its coarseness and brutality.

Anne escaped the hardships of the Clergy Daughters' School at Cowan Bridge, and was educated at home by her father and aunt. She experienced her first formal schooling in 1835 when she replaced Emily as a pupil at Roe Head School, Mirfield.

Describing Anne at the time of their first meeting in 1833, Ellen Nussey wrote:

> dear, gentle Anne, was quite different in appearance from the others ... Her hair was a very pretty light brown and fell on her neck in graceful curls. She had lovely violet blue eyes, fine pencilled eye-brows, a clear, almost transparent complexion.

The publisher George Smith recalled Anne as a 'gentle, quiet, rather subdued person, by no means pretty yet of a pleasing appearance. Her manner was curiously expressive of a wish for protection and encouragement.' In a letter of 1842 Charlotte described her father's young curate, William Weightman, sitting opposite Anne in church, sighing softly '& looking out of the corners of his eyes to win her attention – & Anne is so quiet, her look so downcast.' A few months later Weightman died from cholera at the age of twenty-six. Shortly after his death Anne wrote a poem, 'I will not mourn thee, lovely one', which has led many biographers to assume that Anne loved Weightman.

Anne is distinguished from her sisters by her greater success in making her way in the world of work. Whereas Charlotte managed only two months as a governess in 1839 and ten months in 1841, and Emily lasted only six months as a teacher in a Halifax school, Anne spent nine months

in her first post as governess in the Ingham household at Blake Hall, Mirfield, and five years in her second, as governess to the elder daughters of the Robinsons at Thorp Green Hall, Little Ouseburn, near York.

Three years after she left the second post, the Robinson girls visited their former governess at Haworth. Charlotte observed that they were 'clinging round her like two children', and that they continued to write to Anne 'almost daily'. Of the elder Robinson girl, Charlotte wrote, 'Anne does her best to cheer and counsel her and she seems to cling to her quiet, former governess as her only true friend.' It seems that Anne transferred some aspects of her pupil's character to Rosalie Murray in her first novel, *Agnes Grey* (1847): Rosalie is a flighty, selfish girl who nevertheless recognizes the quiet strength of her governess. Anne recorded in her diary paper that while at Thorp Green she had 'had some very unpleasant and undreamt of experience of human nature'. This also found its way into *Agnes Grey* and her second novel *The Tenant of Wildfell Hall* (1848).

Although Anne is often thought of as the 'dear, gentle Anne' described by Ellen Nussey, she had a remarkable fortitude in life, which compelled her to write with power and truth in her novels. Charlotte commented in a letter that Anne was 'of a remarkably taciturn, still, thoughtful nature, reserved even with her nearest of kin'. Anne's strength of character was never more apparent than in this letter written to Ellen Nussey shortly after Emily's death, when her own

LEFT *A portrait of Anne by her sister Charlotte, dated 17 April 1833. Three portraits of Anne by Charlotte survive, including two watercolours and this pencilled profile, in which Anne poses with a veil over her hair in the manner of a classical goddess. Anne is in fact the most depicted of the Brontës, perhaps because she was the most compliant model.*

ABOVE *Little Ouseburn Church, which Anne and Branwell attended with the Robinsons. Anne made a sketch of the church in the early 1840s.*

illness had been diagnosed as consumption. In it she discusses her wish to travel to the coast in the hope that the sea air would restore her health:

I have no horror of death; if I thought it inevitable I think I could quietly resign myself to the prospect, in the hope that you, dear Miss Nussey, would give as much of your company as you possibly could to Charlotte and be a sister to her in my stead. But I wish it would please God to spare me not only for Papa's and Charlotte's sakes, but because I long to do some good in the world before I leave it. I have many schemes in my head for future practise – humble and limited indeed – but I should not like them all to come to nothing, and myself to have lived to so little purpose. But God's will be done.

ABOVE LEFT *A number of drawings Anne made during her years working as a governess could be interpreted as symbolic images of important stages in her own life. For example, the female figure represented peering out of the wood in* WHAT YOU PLEASE *could be a self-portrait of 1840, depicting Anne on the edge of new opportunities.*

ABOVE *On 7 January 1849 Anne began writing 'Last Lines', a poem expressing her anguish and fear at the prospect of death. The poem reveals great courage in coming to terms with the injustice of her fate. When the poem was published posthumously in 1850, Charlotte edited it by deleting several stanzas, effectively making Anne seem more accepting of death. Anne's manuscript reveals her battle with powerful feelings of anger, and thus a greater strength than Charlotte allowed the world to see.*

ANNE BRONTË

Anne survived Emily by only five months. On 24 May 1849, accompanied by Charlotte and Ellen Nussey, she set out for Scarborough, a place to which she had become attached during summers there with the Robinsons. She died four days later at their lodgings at 2 St Nicholas Cliff. Charlotte described Anne's death in a letter to a friend: 'She died without severe struggle, resigned, trusting in God – thankful for release from a suffering life – deeply assured that a better existence lay before her. She believed, she hoped – and declared her belief and hope with her last breath.'

To spare her father the anguish of another family funeral, Charlotte took the decision to bury her last, much-loved sister in Scarborough. She was laid to rest in the churchyard of St Mary's, high above the town – the only member of the Brontë family not to have been buried in the vault beneath the floor of Haworth church. On returning home afterwards, Charlotte wrote:

> I felt that the house was all silent – the rooms were all empty – I remembered where the three were laid – in what narrow dark dwellings – never were they to reappear on earth … I cannot help thinking of their last days – remembering their sufferings and what they said and did and how they looked in mortal affliction – perhaps all this will become less poignant in time.

THE PARSONAGE SERVANTS

*I now keep two servants but am only to keep one elderly woman now, who,
when my other little girl is at school – will be able to wait I think on my remaining
children and myself.*

PATRICK BRONTË, letter to Mr Mariner, 10 November 1824

There was always at least one live-in servant employed at the Parsonage, for although Mr Brontë was not a wealthy man, female domestic labour came cheap. Before her promotion to housekeeper following Charlotte's death, the family's servant, Martha Brown, earned just £8 a year. When extra help was required, other women were called in: Martha's sisters helped out on occasion, as did a number of other local women, including Hannah Dawson and Sally Mosley, described as 'washing in the back kitchin' in Emily's diary paper for 1834.

NANCY AND SARAH GARRS

Nancy and Sarah Garrs had accompanied the Brontë family from Thornton in 1820. Nancy had joined the family as a nursemaid, but was later promoted to cook and assistant housekeeper. She was replaced in the nursery by her younger sister Sarah following Emily's birth in 1818. The sisters stayed with the family through the sad period of Mrs Brontë's illness and death, leaving shortly before the deaths of Maria and Elizabeth in 1824, when Nancy was to be married.

OPPOSITE *After she and her sister left the Brontës, Nancy Garrs remained in the Bradford area and attended the funerals of both Charlotte and Mr Brontë. She died in the Bradford workhouse, aged eighty-three. Her sister Sarah married William Newsome of Bradford, who emigrated to America in 1841. Sarah followed him with their four children, and died in Iowa City in 1899.*

RIGHT *Martha Wright came to the Parsonage to nurse Mrs Brontë. She later moved to Burnley, Lancashire, returning to the area following her retirement in 1863. She died in 1883, aged ninety-one, and was laid to rest in Haworth churchyard with her husband and her only child, Mary Ann.*

When Mrs Gaskell came to write her biography of Charlotte over thirty years later, she described the Garrs sisters as having been 'wasteful' – a charge they bitterly resented. They appealed to Mr Brontë, who supplied them with a written testimonial: 'I beg leave to state, to all whom it may concern, that Nancy, and Sarah Garrs, during the time they were in my service, were kind to my children, and honest, and not wasteful, but sufficiently careful, in regard to food, and all other articles committed to their charge.'

MARTHA WRIGHT

The story of the wasteful young servants is likely to have been supplied to Mrs Gaskell by Martha Wright, a Haworth woman who came to the Parsonage as Mrs Brontë's nurse. Martha was dismissed for reasons that Mr Brontë thought 'sufficient', and many years later she provided Mrs Gaskell with some colourful tales of his eccentric behaviour that were included in the *Life*. It was Mrs Wright who claimed

that Patrick Brontë refused to allow his children to eat meat and that he cut his wife's silk gown to shreds. Although the Garrs sisters contradicted the stories, her account did much to shape the public image of Patrick Brontë as a stern father, and it continues to be influential today.

TABITHA AYKROYD

The woman employed by Mr Brontë in place of the Garrs sisters was a local woman, Tabitha Aykroyd. It is almost as though her life did not begin until she walked through the Parsonage door, for there are few surviving records to tell us about her early life. 'Tabby', as she was known, was described by Mrs Gaskell as a 'thorough specimen of a Yorkshire woman of her class, in dialect, in appearance and in character … Her words were far from flattery; but she would spare no deeds in the cause of those whom she kindly regarded.' The Parsonage kitchen became Tabby's domain, and here she would chide the children for 'pitter pottering' when there was work to be done. At night they would gather in the fire-lit kitchen to hear her fairy stories and village gossip. It was from Tabby that the children learned the Yorkshire dialect, and she is likely to have been the model for Ellen Dean in *Wuthering Heights*. She must have been a comforting presence to the motherless Brontë children, and became more of a family friend than a servant. She was often referred to in the village

as 'Tabby Brontë', and her gravestone records the fact that she was the faithful servant of the Brontë family for over thirty years.

MARTHA BROWN

Martha Brown, the daughter of John Brown the Sexton, came to the Parsonage at the age of eleven to assist Tabby. 'From my first entering the house,' she later claimed, 'I was always recognised and treated as a member of the family, although by outsiders I was spoken of as "the servant girl".' Like Tabby, Martha remained at the Parsonage for many years, leaving only after Mr Brontë's death in 1861. Patrick Brontë left Martha the sum of thirty pounds, three times her annual salary, as a 'token of regard for long and faithful services to me and my children'.

OPPOSITE *A view of the churchyard from the window in the servants' room.*

LEFT *After the deaths of the Brontës, Martha Brown remained on friendly terms with Charlotte's husband, Arthur Bell Nicholls, corresponding with him and visiting him in Ireland. Nicholls tried to persuade her to make her home there: 'I fear that Haworth does not agree with you, as it is cold & damp. I wish you could make up your mind to live with us, I don't mean as a servant; but to make this your home.' Martha always returned to Haworth and died there in 1880, at the age of fifty-one. She was buried with her parents in the churchyard, close to the south wall of the Parsonage garden.*

THE WORK
OF THE
BRONTËS

LEFT '... her native hills were far more to her than
a spectacle; they were what she lived in, and by,
as much as the wild birds, their tenants, or as the heather,
their produce.' Charlotte Brontë, PREFACE TO
WUTHERING HEIGHTS, 1850

ABOVE Cotton grass on Haworth Moor.

THE ART OF THE BRONTËS

*It is singular how strong a yearning the whole family had toward the art of drawing …
the girls themselves loved everything connected with it – all descriptions of engravings of
great pictures; and, in default of good ones, they would take and analyse any print or
drawing which came their way.*

ELIZABETH GASKELL, *The Life of Charlotte Brontë*, 1857

The many surviving drawings and paintings produced by the young Brontës attest to their early interest in art. Charlotte in particular was passionate about art, and her school friend Mary Taylor claimed that she 'knew much about celebrated pictures and painters. Whenever an opportunity offered of examining a picture or cut of any kind, she went over it piecemeal, with her eyes close to the paper, looking so long that we used to ask her "what she saw in it." She could always see plenty, and explained it very well.'

At the age of thirteen Charlotte drew up a 'list of painters whose works I wish to see'. Her knowledge of these artists was confined to descriptions she had read and the black-and-white engravings she had seen reproduced in periodicals and books. It was to be many years before she got the chance to see great works of art at first hand. During her time as a student teacher in Brussels she took full advantage of the opportunity to visit the city's art galleries, and Mary remembered how she 'picked up every scrap of information concerning painting, sculpture, poetry, music, etc., as if it were gold'. Charlotte held exalted notions regarding the status of the artist: painters frequently figure as important characters in her early writing, and art is a recurrent theme in her published novels.

It is thought that the young Brontës probably had lessons from a local painter, John Bradley, though much of their art training consisted of copying engravings in books. The Brontë girls were encouraged to copy flowers and picturesque scenes, while their brother, before progressing to lessons with the distinguished Leeds artist William Robinson, worked 'from nature'. As they grew older, both Emily and Anne followed suit; although they never painted in oils, they sketched the world around them. Charlotte left a handful of portraits, and often added a touch of her own to the engravings she copied, but she never produced the works of the imagination that she ascribes to Jane Eyre.

Emily seems to have had little interest in copying illustrations in books. Since she showed contempt when it was suggested that she could improve her French compositions by attempting to emulate the style of a great writer, it seems unlikely that she would have been any more sympathetic to the notion of imitation as an effective method

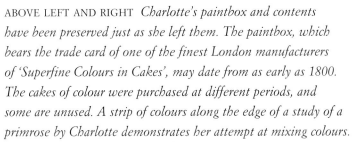

ABOVE LEFT AND RIGHT *Charlotte's paintbox and contents have been preserved just as she left them. The paintbox, which bears the trade card of one of the finest London manufacturers of 'Superfine Colours in Cakes', may date from as early as 1800. The cakes of colour were purchased at different periods, and some are unused. A strip of colours along the edge of a study of a primrose by Charlotte demonstrates her attempt at mixing colours.*

RIGHT *A pencil drawing by Emily, dated January 1834, of Grasper, one of the Parsonage dogs.*

of art training. Emily responded to the natural world, and among the handful of works she left behind are several striking and original drawings of her beloved animals.

Art was one of the essential tools of the governess's trade, but it was also a source of pleasure to Anne. During her time as governess at Thorp Green Hall she spent some of her precious free time making sketches in the grounds. Her first novel, *Agnes Grey*, tells the story of a young governess and contains several references to her attempts to teach drawing to her pupils. In her second novel, *The Tenant of Wildfell Hall*, Anne made a professional woman artist the heroine of her book.

Charlotte apparently even considered a career as a professional artist. She exhibited two of her drawings in the summer exhibition of the Royal

Northern Society for the Encouragement of the Fine Arts in Leeds when she was just eighteen years old. Art, along with music, needlework and French, was considered to be a desirable feminine accomplishment, but not a suitable profession. Women were barred from membership of the Royal Academy of Arts in London. Although it was hoped that Branwell would one day go to study there, he lacked self-discipline and it is difficult to imagine how he would have survived the intensive academic training after the freedom of his childhood. Jane Sellars, who has made a study of Branwell's art, describes him as an artist of 'the immediate response' and believes that 'had he lived just over one hundred years later Branwell would have flourished in a British art college of the 1960s'.

Most of Branwell's surviving work dates from the period when he made a brief attempt to create a career for himself as a portrait painter: portraits in oils of Haworth associates and the sons of Bradford mill owners. When he decided that his true vocation lay in literary composition, his drawing skills were reserved for illustrating letters to friends with grimly humorous sketches that form a pictorial record of his decline into addiction and despair.

In 1848 Charlotte was asked by her publishers to illustrate a second edition of *Jane Eyre*. She declined the offer, having by this time come to a more realistic assessment of her own artistic training and ability:

OPPOSITE ABOVE RIGHT *The Brontës made frequent copies from the wood engravings of Thomas Bewick. The family owned a copy of Bewick's illustrated* HISTORY OF BRITISH BIRDS *and his woodcut vignettes of seascapes, shipwrecks and lonely moonlit churchyards were a source of fascination to them. This pencil drawing by Charlotte is reminiscent of the opening chapter of* JANE EYRE, *in which Jane loses herself in images of 'the haunts of sea-fowl; of the 'solitary rocks and promontories' by them only inhabited ... the rock standing up alone in a sea of billow and spray'.*

OPPOSITE ABOVE LEFT *A pencil drawing by Anne, dated 13 November 1839.*

OPPOSITE *This drawing of a woman feeding a parrot on a parterre is one of five miniature drawings by Charlotte acquired by the Brontë Society in 2004.*

RIGHT *Margaret Hartley, aged thirteen in the late 1830s when this portrait was painted, was the niece of Mr and Mrs Isaac Kirby of Bradford. Branwell lodged with the Kirbys while working as a portraitist, taking a room in their house as a studio. This is one of his most accomplished oil paintings. Reminiscing about him in 1893, the sitter described him as 'a very steady young gentleman, his conduct was exemplary and we liked him very much'.*

It is not enough to have the artist's eye, one must also have the artist's hand to turn the first gift to practical account ... when I examine the contents of my portfolio now, it seems as if during the years it has been lying closed some fairy has changed what I once thought sterling coin into dry leaves, and I feel much inclined to consign the whole collection of drawings to the fire.

Fortunately many of the drawings and paintings by the Brontës have survived and are still mostly to be seen at the Brontë Parsonage Museum. The Brontës are of course famous for their writing rather than their drawing, but the time spent laboriously copying pictures was put to good effect: their novels are rich in picturesque description, for their early habit of drawing and 'reading' pictures honed their powers of observation and fed into their mature writing.

THE BRONTËS' EARLY WRITINGS

The Gondals still flourish bright as ever I am at present writing a work
on the First War – Anne has been writing some articles on this and a book
by Henry Sophona – We intend sticking firm by the rascals as long as they
delight us which I am glad to say they do at present.

EMILY BRONTË, 30 July 1845

While collecting material for her *Life of Charlotte Brontë*, Elizabeth Gaskell visited Charlotte's father and widower at the Parsonage, and during the visit she was handed what she describes as

> a packet about the size of a lady's travelling writing case, full of paper books of different sizes … all in this indescribably fine writing. Mr Gaskell says they would make more than 50 vols of print, but they are the wildest & most incoherent things … They give one the idea of creative power carried to the verge of insanity.

These were the early writings of Charlotte and Branwell Brontë, and Elizabeth Gaskell was probably the first person outside the family circle to read them. Among the manuscripts was one entitled 'The History of the Year', written by Charlotte on 12 March 1829, in which she vividly describes the event that sparked the beginning of their early stories:

> Papa bought Branwell some soldiers at Leeds when papa came home it was night and we where in Bed so next morning Branwell came to our Door with a Box of soldiers

Emily and I jumped out of Bed and I snathed up one and exclaimed this is the Duke of Wellington it shall be mine!! When I said this Emily likewise took one also. Mine was the prettiest of the whole and perfect in every part Emily's was a Grave Looking ferllow we called him Gravey Anne's was a queer little thing very much like herself. He was called waiting Boy Branwell chose Bonaparte.

The children had soon created a sequence of plays around the toy soldiers, or the Twelves, as they became known. These were the 'Young Men's Play', 'Our Fellows Play' and 'The Islanders Play'. The Twelves and their imaginary kingdom were presided over by the children in the guise of four powerful genii, known as Brannii, Tallii, Emmii and Annii.

From acting out stories and plays, it came naturally to the young Brontës to record the events taking place in their imaginary worlds in writing. They produced miniature books and magazines, intended to be 'read' by the toy soldiers, and then hand-stitched them into covers made from scraps of wallpaper or even old sugar bags. The books contained contents pages and advertisements and were intended to resemble the printed magazines that came into the Parsonage. Some of the little books are as small as 36 x 55mm, and their proportionately tiny script makes

LEFT *'A Day at Parry's Palace' by fourteen-year-old Charlotte, writing as Lord Charles Wellesley. In a scene reminiscent of* WUTHERING HEIGHTS, *Lord Charles is abandoned with little Eater, Parry's son. Lord Charles says that the child 'stood for more than half an hour on the rug before me, with his finger in his mouth staring idiot like full in my face'. Irritated beyond endurance, Lord Charles viciously strikes him with a poker, dashing his head upon the floor. Drawn by the child's screams, the entire household arrives on the scene. 'What hauve dou biinn douing tou de child,' demands Parry, advancing towards Lord Charles. 'As I wished to stop a day longer at this palace I was forced to coin a lie. "nothing [at] all" I replied "the sweet little boy fell down as I was playing with him & hurt hisself" this satisfied the good easy man & they all retired carrying the hateful brat still squalling & bawling along with them.'*

ABOVE RIGHT *Charlotte's 'The History of the Year' was written on 12 March 1829 and tells of Mr Brontë's gift of a set of toy soldiers to Branwell and the 'plays' that they inspired.*

them difficult to read without the aid of a magnifying glass. Their size had the advantage of saving paper and would also have acted as a deterrent to the prying eyes of the Parsonage adults.

Branwell inspired many of his sisters' plays and stories, vying with Charlotte in the creation and development of the characters and events taking place in their shared world of Angria. Branwell's main character and alter ego was Alexander Percy, also known as Northangerland, Rogue and Ellrington, while Charlotte concerned herself with Percy's archenemy, the aristocratic villain Zamorna. The Brontës' early writings are full of echoes of their reading and descriptions of both these characters evoke a Byronic hero, 'bright with beauty, dark with crime'.

Growing numbers of chief men, based on contemporary heroes and villains, were added to the plays, and soon Emily's and Anne's soldiers, Gravey and Waiting Boy, had metamorphosed into Sir Edward Parry and Sir John Ross, the real-life Arctic explorers. An article written by Charlotte for the *Young Men's Magazine* of October 1830 describes a visit by her character Lord Charles Wellesley to Sir Edward Parry's Land. Charlotte revelled in written descriptions of sumptuous settings and grand palaces, and her account of Parry's Land pokes fun at her younger sisters' more homely creation. Parry's Palace, square and stone-built, with a garden of 'moderate

ABOVE *Charlotte's copy of* THE ATHEIST VIEWING THE DEAD BODY OF HIS WIFE *by A.B. Clayton. Although it is faithful to the original, she made some small changes to transform it into an image of the deathbed of Mary Percy, Queen of Angria.*

RIGHT *Branwell's portrait of the Angrian character Zamorna. In the Glasstown saga Zamorna was the eldest son of the Duke of Wellington, before he was made Duke of Zamorna and King of Angria.*

dimensions', bears a close resemblance to Haworth Parsonage. Even the meals dished up within its walls sound like the ones eaten by the Brontës. Napkins are worn at mealtimes to protect best clothes, and in contrast to the costly silks and jewels worn by the Angrians, the women of Parry's Land wear brown stuff gowns and plain white caps.

It was while Charlotte was away at school that Emily and Anne took advantage of her absence and broke away to from their own land of Gondal. In her diary paper for 1837 Emily records that she was working on 'Agustus Almedas life 1st vol', but what happened to this volume, and to the other Gondal manuscripts produced by Emily and Anne, can only be surmised. The few surviving clues to Gondal are

to be found in the poetry produced by both sisters, in a list of Gondal place names added to the back of their grammar book and in the brief references contained in their diary papers. As late as 1845 the sisters, by then aged nearly twenty-seven and twenty-five, were still absorbed by the Gondal saga. Emily's diary paper for that year reveals how

BELOW LEFT *'The Monthly Intelligencer', a miniature newspaper produced by Branwell between 27 March and 26 April 1833.*

BELOW RIGHT *A portrait by Charlotte believed to be of Branwell's Angrian alter ego, Alexander Percy, Duke of Northangerland.*

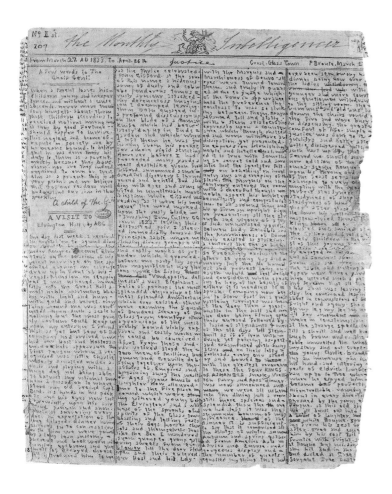

on a journey to York she and Anne 'played' at being Gondal characters:

> Anne and I went our first long journey by ourselves … during our excursion we were Ronald Macelgin, Henry Angora, Juliet Augusteena, Rosobelle Esraldan, Ella and Julian Egramont Catherine Navarre and Cordelia Fitzaphnold escaping from the Palaces of Instruction to join the Royalists who are hard driven at present by the victorious Republicans.

Emily rarely left home and the themes of her adult writing carry on seamlessly from those of her youth. Although Anne appears to have been less overwhelmed by the fantasy world than her siblings, the character Huntingdon in her second published novel, like Emily's Heathcliff and Charlotte's Rochester, owes a great deal to Angrian and Gondal characters.

In a diary fragment for 1839, known as 'Farewell to Angria', Charlotte wrote of her determination to break free from her fantasy world and how it was 'no easy theme

to dismiss from my imagination, the images which have filled it so long'. Her first attempts to write a novel for publication reflect this difficulty and the opening chapters of her novel *The Professor* contain Angrian names and situations transposed to a Yorkshire setting. Branwell also attempted to tear himself away from Angria, but long immersion in a fantasy world had left him unfit for real life. The doomed love affairs and guilty passions that pervade the Brontës' early writings were, to some extent, lived out by Branwell and re-enacted in his relationship with the wife of his employer, Mrs Robinson. Unlike his sisters, he was never able to make something constructive from the Angrian experience.

The story of treachery and deception involved in the fate of the Brontës' surviving manuscripts reads like the plot of a novel. After the deaths of all the Brontës, their papers passed into the hands of Charlotte's husband, Arthur Bell Nicholls. For forty years they remained in a brown-paper bundle before being sold to a collector, Thomas J. Wise. Despite Wise's reputation as a respected bibliographer and his assurances that the manuscripts were destined for a national collection, he soon had the little scraps in their rough paper covers handsomely bound and sold them on to wealthy collectors in England and America. Works by Branwell were attributed to his more collectable sister Charlotte, causing confusion over authorship that has persisted almost to the present day.

The difficulty in locating manuscripts and the task of deciphering the minute handwriting have meant that it is only relatively recently that scholars have been able to piece together the narratives of Glasstown and Angria, and that definitive editions of both Charlotte's and Branwell's works have been published. A study of the Brontës' early writing reveals the shared influences from which their writing springs and makes clear the fact that the published novels of the three sisters did not emerge from nowhere: Charlotte, Emily and Anne had served a long apprenticeship as writers.

LEFT *According to Mrs Gaskell, the servants called this room the 'children's study' because it was here that the young Brontës would read and develop their imaginary worlds.*

RIGHT *The window of the children's study is directly above the front door of the Parsonage, looking out on to the melancholy churchyard.*

POEMS

You evidently possess & in no inconsiderable degree what Wordsworth calls "the faculty of Verse." I am not deprecating it when I say that in these times it is not rare … Literature cannot be the business of a woman's life: & it ought not to be. The more she is engaged in her proper duties, the less leisure will she have for it, even as an accomplishment & a recreation. To those duties you have not yet been called, & when you are you will be less eager for celebrity.

ROBERT SOUTHEY, letter to Charlotte Brontë, 12 March 1837

In 1836, at the age of twenty, Charlotte wrote to the ageing Poet Laureate, Robert Southey, to ask for an opinion on her poems. Her letter has not survived, but Southey's reply makes it clear that she had told him of her desire 'to be for ever known' as a poet. Although Southey took the trouble to respond to Charlotte's letter, his advice was not encouraging. Charlotte kept Southey's letter, informing him that she would 'never more feel ambitious to see my name in print' and that 'if the wish should arise, I'll look at Southey's letter, and suppress it.' Charlotte kept the letter for the rest of her life but fortunately she did not follow the advice.

In the *Biographical Notice of Ellis and Acton Bell*, published in the 1850 edition of *Wuthering Heights* and *Agnes Grey*, Charlotte recounts how the Brontë sisters came to publish their poems:

RIGHT *Sheep on Haworth Moor in winter.*

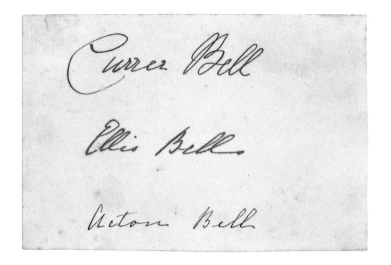

One day, in the autumn of 1845, I accidentally lighted on a MS. volume of verse in my sister Emily's handwriting. Of course, I was not surprised, knowing that she could and did write verse: I looked it over, and something more than surprise seized me, – a deep conviction that these were not common effusions, nor at all like the poetry women generally write. I thought them condensed and terse, vigorous and genuine. To my ear, they had also a peculiar music – wild, melancholy, and elevating.

Anne had also written poetry, and Charlotte found that 'these verses too had a sweet sincere pathos of their own.' That was when she became convinced that there was enough material to publish a slim volume of poetry by all three sisters and, despite Emily's fury at the invasion of her privacy, eventually won them round to the idea of publication. Branwell was not included in the project, despite the fact that he had already seen several of his poems published in local newspapers. Having been dismissed from his post at Thorp Green in the previous year he had taken to drinking in earnest; and after his death in 1848, Charlotte told her publisher that her brother never knew of his sisters' publications, and that they could not tell him for fear of causing him 'too deep a pang of remorse for his own time misspent, and talents misapplied'.

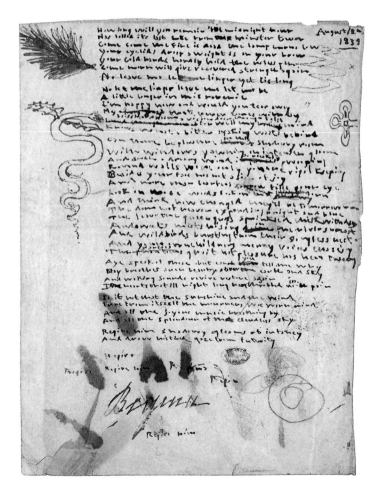

LEFT ABOVE *The signatures of Currer, Ellis and Acton Bell, provided by the Brontës at the request of an early autograph hunter.*

LEFT BELOW *The manuscript of Emily's poem 'How long will you remain?', dated 12 August 1839.*

RIGHT *A weather-sculpted moorland tree.*

The sisters agreed that their poems would be published under pseudonyms. In her *Biographical Notice*, Charlotte explained their reasons for this:

> Averse to personal publicity, we veiled our own names under those of Currer, Ellis and Acton Bell; the ambiguous choice being dictated by a sort of conscientious scruple at assuming Christian names positively masculine, while we did not like to declare ourselves women, because – without at that time suspecting that our mode of writing and thinking was not what is called 'feminine' – we had a vague impression that authoresses are liable to be looked on with prejudice.

Poems by Currer, Ellis and Acton Bell was published by Aylott and Jones in 1846, in a print run of 1,000 copies at the sisters' own expense. The poems chosen by Anne for inclusion in the volume are often religious in theme, reflecting the influence of William Cowper, one of her favourite poets. Charlotte was disparaging about her own contribution, later describing her poems as 'chiefly juvenile productions'. Emily's are by far the most powerful, and of a similar tone to *Wuthering Heights*.

The superiority of Ellis Bell's contribution to the 1846 volume was discerned by the critic for the *Athenaeum*. He described the Bells as 'a family in whom appears to run the instinct of song'; that instinct

> is shared, however, by the three brothers – as we suppose them to be – in very unequal proportions; requiring in the case of Acton Bell, the indulgences of affection … and rising, in that of Ellis, into an inspiration, which may yet find an audience in the outer world. A fine quaint spirit has the latter, which may have things to speak that men will be glad to hear, – and an evident power of wing that may reach heights not here attempted.

A reviewer in the *Critic* praised the poems as possessing 'more genius than it was supposed this utilitarian age had devoted to the loftier exercises of the intellect'. This was heady praise for unknown authors, but despite the favourable reviews, only two copies of *Poems* sold. After a year the sisters sent some of the unsold copies to authors they admired. In a note accompanying one of these copies, Charlotte wrote:

> My relatives Ellis & Acton Bell and myself, heedless of the repeated warnings of various respectable publishers, have committed the rash act of printing a volume of poems … our book is found to be a drug; no man needs it or heeds it; in the space of a year our publisher has disposed but of two copies and by what painful efforts he succeeded in getting rid of those two – himself only knows.

'Ill success failed to crush us,' wrote Charlotte, adding that 'the mere effort to succeed had given a wonderful zest to existence: it must be pursued.' The sisters set to work and launched into their next literary venture – novel writing.

JANE EYRE

We do not hesitate to say that the tone of the mind and the thought which has overthrown authority and violated every code human and divine abroad, and fostered Chartism and rebellion at home, is the same which has also written Jane Eyre.

ELIZABETH RIGBY'S UNSIGNED REVIEW IN THE *Quarterly Review*, December 1848

When Charlotte's first attempt at writing a novel for publication, *The Professor*, was rejected by Smith, Elder & Co., the publisher sent Charlotte a letter which she considered 'discussed its merits and demerits so courteously … that this very refusal cheered the author better than a vulgarly-expressed acceptance would have done. It was added, that a work in three volumes would meet with careful attention.'

Charlotte was already working on another manuscript, and on 24 August 1847, only a month after the publisher had written, she posted *Jane Eyre* by rail from Keighley. George Smith, the head of the firm, later recounted the effect the book had on him:

> After breakfast on Sunday morning I took the MS. of Jane Eyre to my little study, and began to read it. The story quickly took me captive … Presently the servant came to tell me that luncheon was ready; I asked him to bring me a sandwich and a glass of wine, and still went on with Jane Eyre. Dinner came; for me the meal was a very hasty one, and before I went to bed that night I had finished reading the manuscript.

Smith accepted the book and offered Charlotte one hundred pounds for the copyright. *Jane Eyre* appeared on 19 October 1847 and its sensational popularity marked a turning point in the fortunes of both author and publisher: Charlotte became one of the most acclaimed authors of her day, while George Smith went on to become one of the most successful publishers.

In writing *Jane Eyre*, Charlotte drew on incidents from her own life, infused with elements of the supernatural and the fairy tale. She interwove memories of places and houses she had known with her fictional creation, and recreated Cowan Bridge, the charitable school where she and her

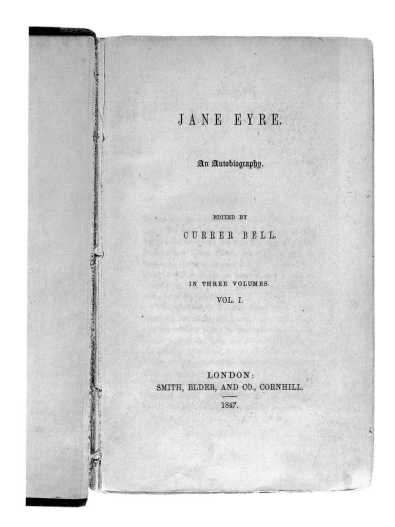

sisters had suffered twenty years before, as Lowood, the infamous school to which Jane is sent in the early chapters of the book. Charlotte wrote with a passionate emotional intensity, and all her rage and sense of injustice at the cruelty of her sisters' treatment there found expression in the novel.

OPPOSITE *A spectacular sky over the upper Worth Valley. Both Charlotte and Emily use fiery evening skies and other elements of the natural world in their writing to heighten human states of being.*

ABOVE *A first edition of* JANE EYRE, *published in 1847.*

The gripping story and charged language transport the reader from Lowood to Thornfield Hall, where Jane becomes governess to the ward of Mr Rochester. As the story unfolds, the descriptions of the hall take on a more sinister, Gothic aspect with resonances of Bluebeard's castle, preparing us for the events that are to come. Jane and Rochester share a passionate nature but, as with all Byronic heroes, Rochester has a dark secret. On the morning that Jane is to marry him, she learns of his mad wife Bertha, kept under lock and key in the Thornfield attic.

THE MAD WOMAN IN THE ATTIC

The figure of the mad woman is rife in nineteenth-century fiction, for the Victorians were preoccupied by notions of insanity and the realms of excess. Uncontrolled passion was seen as leading to degeneracy and madness, the truth of which must have struck Charlotte forcibly when she witnessed the terrible results of her brother Branwell's guilty passion for his employer's wife. In the novel we are told that Bertha's excesses have led to the premature development of 'the germs of insanity'. There is also a suggestion in the text that her racial background is a factor in her degeneracy and madness, for she has grown up amidst the luxury, idleness and corruption of a society based on slave ownership.

Jane strives throughout the novel to assert her self-control and become the kind of 'disciplined and subdued character' exemplified by her former teacher, Miss Temple. The alternation of self-control and rebellion are expressed as a pattern embodied in the novel's use of alternating images of fire and ice. In Sandra Gilbert and Susan Gubar's well-known interpretation of the novel, Bertha functions as Jane's 'darkest double ... the ferocious secret self Jane has been trying to repress ever since her days at Gateshead'.

Bertha, it is said, carries out the things that Jane herself secretly wishes to do.

If Bertha is seen as Jane's 'darkest double', she could also be seen as a symbol of Rochester's own degraded and dangerous nature. Bertha and Rochester are physically alike; Jane tells us that Bertha is a 'big woman, in stature almost equalling her husband'. In confining Bertha to the attic, Rochester could almost be trying to subdue his own passionate nature. That he is not always successful is represented by Bertha's liability to break out of her prison.

Charlotte would have been aware of several instances of mad women being confined within remote houses – one of them within her father's parish. Joseph Greenwood of Springhead, on the outskirts of Haworth, was well known to the Brontës, and for several years his daughter was incarcerated in an upstairs room of the house. Conditions in asylums were notoriously inhumane in the earlier part of the nineteenth century, leading to many 'lunatics' being cared for at home, their existence kept as a shameful secret. Further afield, it is possible that during her time as governess to the Sidgwick family at Stonegappe, Lothersdale, Charlotte visited Norton Conyers, a gloomy, atmospheric house near Ripon, with its own legend of a mad woman imprisoned in the attic. Although there are no references to Norton Conyers in Charlotte's surviving letters, Charlotte's friend Ellen Nussey remembered 'receiving from Charlotte Brontë a verbal description of the place and recalled the impression made on Charlotte by the story of the mad woman confined to the attic'.

The picturesque ruins of Wycoller Hall, just over the border in Lancashire. The hall was thought to be the model for Ferndean Manor, the secluded house to which Rochester retreats after Thornfield is destroyed by fire in JANE EYRE.

for Thornfield. Charlotte had first visited Rydings in 1832. Although the exterior of the house has been preserved, the environment has not. The ancient trees and bluebell woods have long since made way for the Leeds to Huddersfield road. Erskine Stuart, writing in the late 1880s, was in a better position to see the house as Charlotte had known it. Although even at that time the mill chimneys were closing in, Stuart could still claim that Rydings 'is a beautifully situated residence in the castellated style, standing on an eminence outside Birstall. In Charlotte Brontë's word-picture of Thornfield in *Jane Eyre*, we have the description of this building given to the life.'

CRITICAL RECEPTION

The novel was instantly popular with the reading public and has sustained that popularity ever since. Reviews were favourable at first, but a Victorian novel that was outspoken in its treatment of religious and social injustice was guaranteed to provoke a certain amount of adverse critical comment. In the following year, the sentiments expressed anonymously by Elizabeth Rigby in the *Quarterly Review* gained some currency.

It has generally been accepted that parts of *Jane Eyre* are set in the Derbyshire area, which Charlotte visited with Ellen Nussey in 1845. One of the contenders for the original of Thornfield Hall is the romantic-looking North Lees Hall at Hathersage, a castellated manor house that was owned by the Eyre family. Ellen Nussey, however, believed that her own old home, Rydings, at Birstall, provided the inspiration

Her view that the book was an 'anti-Christian composition' was taken up by other critics. 'To say that *Jane Eyre* is positively immoral or anti-Christian, would be to do its writer an injustice,' commented the *Christian Remembrancer*, but 'still it wears a questionable aspect'. It is difficult for modern readers to understand the shocked reactions of *Jane Eyre*'s first critics: Charlotte was a clergyman's daughter and her heroine possesses a powerful moral sense of right and wrong. It is notable, however, that representatives of the established Church portrayed in Charlotte's novels are described in terms of stone and chill,

and are all, without exception, shown to be deeply flawed human beings. One early critic went so far as to claim that Charlotte's writing revealed 'an intimate acquaintance with the worst parts of human nature'.

Charlotte addressed some of her critics in a preface she wrote for the second edition of *Jane Eyre*. She also took the opportunity to dedicate the book to W.M. Thackeray, a novelist whose works she very much admired. She would surely have been delighted by his verdict on her work; for after having been sent a copy of the novel, Thackeray wrote to George Smith:

> I wish you had not sent me Jane Eyre. It interested me so much that I have lost (or won if you like) a whole day in reading it at the busiest period, with the printers I know waiting for copy. Who the author can be I can't guess – if a woman she knows her language better than most ladies do, or has had a 'classical' education. It is a fine book though – the man & woman capital – the style very generous and upright so to speak … Some of the love passages made me cry – to the astonishment of John who came in with the coals … I don't know why I tell you this but that I have been exceedingly moved & pleased by Jane Eyre.

OPPOSITE ABOVE *Norton Conyers, just north of Ripon, is sometimes claimed as a model for Thornfield in* JANE EYRE.

OPPOSITE BELOW *Using information from Ellen Nussey, E.M. Wimperis based his illustration of Thornfield Hall on Rydings.*

ABOVE *The Apostles' cupboard belonging to the Eyre family of North Lees Hall, Hathersage. Jane Eyre observes such a cupboard in flickering candlelight as she keeps watch over the wounded Mr Mason in the Thornfield attic: 'a great cabinet … whose front, divided into twelve panels, bore in grim design, the heads of the twelve apostles, each inclosed in its separate panel as in a frame'.*

Another admirer of *Jane Eyre* was G.H. Lewes, whom Charlotte had met on one of her visits to London. In his review for *Fraser's Magazine* he wrote:

> No such book has gladdened our eyes for a long while. Almost all that we require in a novelist she has: perception of character, and power of delineating it; picturesqueness; passion; and knowledge of life. The story is not only of singular interest, naturally evolved, unflagging to the last, but it fastens itself upon your attention, and will not leave you. The book closed, the enchantment continues.

WUTHERING HEIGHTS

If we did not know that this book has been read by thousands of young ladies in the country, we should esteem it our first duty to caution them against it simply on account of the coarseness of the style.

Review of WUTHERING HEIGHTS, *American Review*, June 1848

The Brontë sisters collaborated in the writing of their novels and would discuss their writing and read portions of their work aloud. It seems unlikely, however, that Emily ever adopted her sisters' suggestions: Charlotte recalled how:

> If the auditor of her work when read in manuscript, shuddered under the grinding influence of natures so relentless and implacable, of spirits so lost and fallen; if it was complained that the mere hearing of certain vivid and fearful scenes banished sleep by night, and disturbed mental peace by day, Ellis Bell would wonder what was meant, and suspect the complainant of affectation.

By July 1846 Emily had completed *Wuthering Heights*. After several rejections, the London publisher Thomas Cautley Newby accepted it, along with Anne's novel *Agnes Grey* – the first Brontë novels to be accepted for publication – on terms that Charlotte described as 'somewhat impoverishing to the two authors'. It was agreed that the authors would pay the sum of fifty pounds for a print run of 350 copies, and that the money would be refunded when a sufficient number of copies had been sold. (However, their publisher, Thomas Cautley Newby, was a rather unscrupulous character and in the event, only 250 copies of the novels were printed, and it was left to Charlotte to try to reclaim the money after her sisters' deaths.) Most novels were first published in three volumes, a format preferred by the circulating libraries, who were by far the largest purchasers of books. The two novels were therefore to be published together, with *Wuthering Heights* filling the first two volumes and *Agnes Grey* making up the third. After much delay, the two novels appeared in December 1847 as a three-volume set under Emily and Anne's pseudonyms, Ellis and Acton Bell. Charlotte commented in a letter to her own publisher that 'the orthography & punctuation of the books are mortifying to a degree – almost all the errors that were corrected in the proof-sheets appear intact in what should have been fair copies.'

'… the whole hill-back was one billowy, white ocean; the swells and falls not indicating corresponding rises and depressions in the ground: many pits, at least, were filled to a level; and entire ranges of mounds, the refuse of the quarries, blotted out from the chart which my yesterday's walk left pictured in my mind.'
Emily Brontë, WUTHERING HEIGHTS

'A Dark Tale Darkly Told'

Wuthering Heights begins when Mr Earnshaw returns home from a trip to Liverpool with a dark orphan child. The boy is named Heathcliff and brought up with Earnshaw's own children, Hindley and Cathy, at their isolated moorland home, Wuthering Heights. Heathcliff is a cuckoo in the nest and, right from the beginning, brings an element of discord into the lives of the Earnshaws and their nearest neighbours, the Lintons.

The first half of the book deals with the passionate spiritual bond between Heathcliff and Cathy, and ends when Cathy, having married Edgar Linton, dies after giving birth to their child. The second half of the novel is haunted by Heathcliff's sense of loss and his search for vengeance. Heathcliff has mysteriously acquired both wealth and an outward appearance of gentility, which he uses to masterly effect – assisting Hindley Earnshaw to drink himself to death and persuading Edgar's sister, Isabella, to elope with him. In this way the former plough boy gains possession of both Wuthering Heights and the Linton home, Thrushcross Grange. His longing to be reunited with Cathy proves too powerful in the end, and he dies before his revenge is complete.

LITERATURE AND LEGEND

The wild, stormy landscapes of the novel often reflect the tempestuous emotions of the characters. *Wuthering Heights*, with its air of decayed grandeur, owes much to the Gothic novels of the late eighteenth century. The characters in *Wuthering Heights* belong to the fictional world of Gondal and were drawn from Emily's imagination. It became a fixed idea from early on that the remote mansions and wild

settings of all the Brontë novels had real-life counterparts. In the 1870s, when Charlotte's publisher, Smith, Elder & Co., decided to issue the first illustrated edition of the Brontës' novels, the commissioned artist worked from a list of original locations supplied by Charlotte's school friend Ellen Nussey. Ellen Nussey suggested that Top Withens, an isolated farmhouse about four miles from the Parsonage, was the model for Wuthering Heights – an identification that has persisted to the present day. However, although it is possible that Emily had the dramatic setting of Withens

ABOVE *Snow on Stanbury Moor, with Top Withens in the distance. This ruined old farmhouse has entered Brontë mythology as the inspiration for Wuthering Heights in Emily's novel.*

in mind when she wrote her novel, the now derelict house bears little resemblance to the home of the Earnshaws. Clearly the artist, E.M. Wimperis, thought so too; in the engraving he produced, Top Withens has been enlarged and another storey added.

Ponden Hall, lying in a valley about two miles from Haworth, is popularly associated with Thrushcross Grange in the novel, although the house at Ponden is far less grand and bears as much resemblance to the Grange as Top Withens does to the Heights. The seventeenth-century hall was home to generations of the Heaton family, and during the Brontës' time, it was one of the more impressive houses of the area. Tales of past Heaton tragedies, one concerning

BELOW LEFT *Ponden Hall near Stanbury is often suggested as the model for Thrushcross Grange, the home of the Lintons in* WUTHERING HEIGHTS.

BELOW RIGHT *A date plaque above the door of Ponden Hall states that the house was rebuilt by Robert Heaton in 1801, the year, incidentally, that* WUTHERING HEIGHTS *opens.*

an attempted usurpation of the family fortunes by a Heathcliff-like figure named Henry Casson, would have been familiar to the Brontës.

There are several other isolated dwellings in the vicinity of Haworth that correspond, in some respect, to the houses

in the book. With its deep-set mullioned windows, Wuthering Heights resembles many a northern farmhouse. What sets Emily's house apart is its singular facade: 'Before passing the threshold, I paused to admire a quantity of grotesque carving lavished over the front, and especially about the principal door, above which, among a wilderness of crumbling griffins, and shameless little boys, I detected the date "1500" and the name "Hareton Earnshaw".' With this description in mind, it seems much more likely that Emily drew on the appearance of High Sunderland Hall at Southowram, a bleak hilltop parish above Halifax. The entrance to High Sunderland was embellished with ornate stone carvings resembling griffins and, in place of Emily's 'shameless little boys', large, misshapen nude men. Emily would have known this remarkable house from her time as a teacher at Miss Patchett's school at nearby Law Hill in 1838–9. By this date, the former home of the Sunderland

family was occupied by tenant farmers and already falling into a state of decay. It was demolished in 1950.

It was not only the architectural details and settings of these houses that contributed to the novel: Emily was also likely to have known the histories of their former inhabitants. Long after the Brontës' deaths, Ellen Nussey recalled how:

> Mr Brontë at times would relate strange stories which had been told to him by some of the oldest inhabitants in the Parish, of the extraordinary lives and doings of people who resided in far off out of the way places but in contiguity with Haworth – stories which made one shiver and shrink from hearing, but they were full of grim humour & interest to Mr Brontë and his children.

Mr Brontë's stories were supplemented by those of Tabitha Aykroyd, the local woman who gave faithful domestic

High Sunderland Hall was a dramatic-looking seventeenth-century house, standing on an exposed hillside just outside Halifax. Emily would have known the house from her time as a teacher at nearby Law Hill, and it is likely that features of the house came into her mind when she began to write WUTHERING HEIGHTS.

service to the Brontës for over thirty years. According to Mrs Gaskell, Tabby had 'many a tale to tell of by-gone days of the country-side … former inhabitants, decayed gentry, who had melted away, and whose places knew them no more; family tragedies, and dark superstitious dooms'.

CRITICAL RECEPTION

Following the phenomenal success of *Jane Eyre* (though it was accepted for publication after *Wuthering Heights* and *Agnes Grey*, in fact it appeared first), the appearance of another 'Bell' novel was bound to attract notice, and the unscrupulous Newby was quick to capitalize on the Bell connection. Initially, *Wuthering Heights* was only noticed at all because it was thought to be an earlier work by 'Currer Bell'. It was usually compared unfavourably with *Jane Eyre*. *Wuthering Heights*, it was felt, without being 'equal in merit' to *Jane Eyre*, shared a 'distinct family likeness' to it.

One early reviewer found it 'a strange sort of book, – baffling all regular criticism', a verdict that few critics would disagree with. One critic claimed to know 'nothing in the whole range of our fictitious literature which presents such shocking pictures of the worst forms of humanity', and another declared: 'Nothing like it has ever been written before; it is to be hoped that in respect of its faults, for the sake of good manners, nothing will be hereafter.' G.W. Peck, reviewing the book for the *American Review*, considered that the novel's 'profanity' and 'savageness' indicated that 'the writer was not accustomed to the society of gentlemen, and was not afraid, indeed, rather gloried, in showing it.' In reading *Wuthering Heights*, Victorian critics found confirmation of the 'brutalizing influence of unchecked passions', but if this was intended to be the novel's message, it was the only moral that critics were able to extract.

Many of the early reviews express shocked condemnation, often mixed with what amounts to praise of the highest order. One review that deplores the novel's 'ill-mannered contempt for the decencies of language' also confesses to having heard it spoken of as 'next in merit to Shakespeare for depth of insight and dramatic power'. The majority of critics were forced to acknowledge the power of the novel, although E.P. Whipple, writing for the *North American Review*, believed this to be 'power thrown away', for 'Nightmares and dreams, through which devils dance and wolves howl, make bad novels.' This review was read aloud by Charlotte to her sisters just a few weeks before Emily's death. In a letter she wrote:

> As I sat at our quiet but now somewhat melancholy fireside, I studied the two ferocious authors. Ellis the 'man of uncommon talents but dogged, brutal and morose,' sat leaning back in his easy chair drawing his impeded breath as he best could, and looking alas! piteously pale and wasted – it is not his wont to laugh – but he smiled half-amused and half in scorn as he listened.

An early critic predicted that *Wuthering Heights* would 'live a short and brilliant life, and then die and be forgotten … Poor Cathy's ghost will not walk the earth forever; and the insane Heathcliff will soon rest quietly in his coveted repose.' Throughout much of the nineteenth century critics concentrated on Charlotte's work. Late in the century, however, *Wuthering Heights* attracted many enthusiasts, notably the poet Swinburne. In the years since, the novel has been translated into over twenty-five languages and its characters and themes have become part of popular culture. The novel has been adapted many times for stage and television, and has also inspired ballet, opera and musicals.

AGNES GREY

… if Anne Brontë had lived ten years longer she would have taken a place beside Jane Austen, perhaps even a higher place … her first story, AGNES GREY, *is the most perfect prose narrative in English literature.*

GEORGE MOORE, *Conversations in Ebury Street*, 1924

In her diary paper for 31 July 1845, Anne Brontë refers to having begun work on the third volume of a manuscript called *Passages in the Life of an Individual*, which may have been an earlier draft of her first published novel, *Agnes Grey*.

Agnes Grey tells of the trials of a governess's life. The novel has often been read as autobiography, for Agnes, like Anne herself, is the youngest daughter of a 'clergyman of the north of England'. When the family falls on hard times, financial necessity compels Agnes and her sister to earn a living. Agnes decides to go out to work as a governess, a prospect she views enthusiastically as a step towards independence:

> How delightful it would be to be a governess! To go out into the world; to enter upon a new life; to act for myself; to exercise my unused faculties; to try my unknown powers; to earn my own maintenance … to show papa what his little Agnes could do; to convince mama and Mary that I was not quite the helpless, thoughtless being they supposed.

Agnes works as a governess in two households and is quickly disillusioned, finding both sets of pupils spoilt and unmanageable. The novel was coloured by Anne's own experience as a governess, first to the Ingham family of Blake Hall, Mirfield, and then to the Robinson family of Thorp Green Hall near York.

THE VICTORIAN GOVERNESS

The rise of the wealthy manufacturers, particularly in the north of England, created a new middle class, and the task of teaching their daughters fell to the impoverished ladies of the educated classes or the daughters of poor clergymen. The clergyman's daughter, already used to teaching in Sunday schools and usually well bred, quiet and self-effacing, had a certain appeal for the *nouveau riche*. The governess was a social incongruity: because she was middle class she could not be classified as a servant, and because she was poor enough to have to work for her living she could not easily be seen as a friend or treated like a member of the family. She was often submitted to overwork and social humiliation for a very low salary, and once her charges were of marriageable age, she became expendable.

Governesses were primarily entrusted with the education of young ladies. In wealthy families the boys would remain

Blake Hall, Mirfield (now demolished), where Anne Brontë was employed as governess to the Ingham family in 1839. In a letter Anne described her pupils as 'desperate little dunces'. She was not allowed by the parents to discipline the children herself – an impossible situation for any teacher, which she describes with conviction in AGNES GREY.

in the care of the governess only as long as they were infants, after which they would be taught by a male tutor or sent away to school. The main purpose of educating a girl was to make her a more attractive proposition to potential marriage partners; her only sphere was expected to be the home – her father's home before marriage and her husband's afterwards. Serious study was seen as both unnecessary and undesirable for a girl. In *Agnes Grey* Anne describes the qualities Agnes's employer expects her to instil into her pupils:

> For the girls, she seemed anxious only to render them as superficially attractive, and showily accomplished, as they could possibly be made without present trouble or discomfort to themselves … with regard to the two boys it was much the same, only instead of accomplishments, I was to get the greatest possible quantity of Latin grammar and Valpy's Delectus into their heads, in order to fit them for school.

CRITICAL RECEPTION

Anne Brontë's quiet tale of governess life suffered from being published together with Emily's *tour de force*, *Wuthering Heights*, and did not receive the critical attention it might otherwise have done. 'Of *Agnes Grey*, much need not be said,' reported one reviewer, and critical comment on *Agnes Grey* was usually restricted to a few lines tacked on to a lengthy review of *Wuthering Heights*.

It was unfortunate that, although *Agnes Grey* had been written before *Jane Eyre*, Newby's tardiness in publishing it meant that Charlotte's novel appeared first, and Anne's governess tale was seen as a poor imitation of her sister's. '*Agnes Grey* is a tale well worth the writing and reading,' claimed the reviewer for *Douglas Jerrold's Weekly Newspaper*, adding, 'The heroine is a sort of younger sister to Jane Eyre; but inferior to her in every way.'

Anne is usually seen as the least gifted writer of the Brontë family. Mrs Humphrey Ward, writing in 1900, described her works as serving only as 'a matter of comparison by which to test the greatness of her two sisters. She is the measure of their genius – like them, yet not with them.' It was well into the twentieth century before a re-evaluation of Anne's work got under way and led one writer to claim that Anne Brontë 'would have passed for a genius in any other family'.

The secluded, pastoral landscape of the Worth Valley between Stanbury and Oldfield.

THE TENANT OF WILDFELL HALL

… our object in the present paper is to warn our readers, and more especially our lady-readers, against being induced to peruse it, either by the powerful interest of the story, or the talent with which it is written. Did we think less highly of it in these particulars, we should have left the book to its fate.

Unsigned review in *Sharpe's London Magazine*, 1848

Anne Brontë's second novel, *The Tenant of Wildfell Hall*, was published under her pseudonym, Acton Bell, in 1848. In contrast to her first work – a semi-autobiographical account of a governess' life – in *The Tenant*, Anne adopted a more radical, feminist theme.

In the 1840s, when Anne was writing the novel, women were without property rights or legal status. Any property a woman owned on marriage automatically became her husband's, unless costly legal settlements were put in place. Divorce was an option available only to the very rich, and women had no legal rights in relation to their children.

The novel's protagonist, Helen, falls in love with Arthur Huntingdon and marries him against the advice of her relatives. Any hopes she entertained of reforming her rakish husband are quickly dispelled. He squanders much of her

Rush Isles Farm at Ponden on a misty morning.

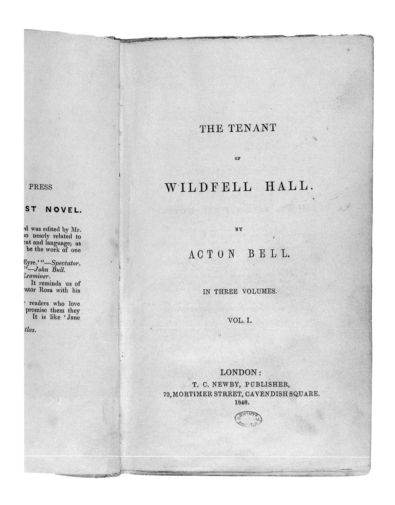

THE TENANT

OF

WILDFELL HALL.

BY

ACTON BELL.

IN THREE VOLUMES.

VOL. I.

LONDON:
T. C. NEWBY, PUBLISHER,
72, MORTIMER STREET, CAVENDISH SQUARE.
1848.

fortune and his corrupting influence begins to take hold of their young son. When Helen runs away from her husband, she uses her skills as a painter to make her living and becomes the mysterious tenant of Wildfell Hall.

Although Huntingdon bears little resemblance to Branwell Brontë, his disintegration was certainly influenced by Anne's brother's decline into alcoholism and disgrace. The novel was also coloured by her long involvement in the fictional worlds she had created with her siblings in childhood. In *The Tenant*, the wild, debauched ways of the Gondal *salons* become those of the English drawing room. Gondal in turn owed much to the works of Lord Byron and Thomas Moore's biography of the poet. Anne appears

to have been less overwhelmed by Byronism than her siblings and disapproved of her sisters' morally corrupt yet devastatingly attractive heroes. The disastrous marriage between Helen and Arthur Huntingdon could easily have been modelled on Byron's scandalous marriage to Annabella Milbanke; Helen's status as an heiress, and her confident hopes of reforming her dissipated husband, closely parallel the situation of Lady Byron.

It would be interesting to know if Anne had access to the writings of Mary Wollstonecraft. *The Tenant* shares a common theme and purpose with Wollstonecraft's *The Wrongs of Woman*, which was published posthumously in 1798. Maria, like Helen, is a serious and intelligent young woman who makes a disastrous marriage. She escapes with her child, only to be captured and placed in an asylum. Here she meets Darnford, and her story takes the form of a written memoir, handed to the man who is ready to love her on achieving their freedom.

Anne Brontë's second novel was not received with enthusiasm by her sister Charlotte: '*Wildfell Hall* it hardly seems to me desirable to preserve,' she wrote to her publisher following the firm's acquisition of the copyright in all the Brontë novels. Charlotte's disapproval kept the novel out of publication for ten years following Anne's death. She disliked the theme of the book and was appalled by the idea of her gentle younger sister having written it – 'the choice of subject was an mistake … nothing less congruous with the writer's nature could be conceived.' She believed that the book was Anne's rather morbid response to having witnessed 'near at hand and for a long time, the terrible effects of talents misused and faculties abused'. She explained Anne's motivation in writing as a duty: 'she believed it to be a duty to reproduce every detail … as a warning to others. She hated her work, but would pursue it.'

WILDFELL HALL

CRITICAL RECEPTION

The novel sold well and quickly went into a second edition, although many readers and reviewers were shocked by its stark depiction of the harrowing effects of alcoholism. *Sharpe's London Magazine* expressed 'deep regret' that the novel should be

> rendered unfit for the perusal of the very class of persons to whom it would be most useful, (namely imaginative girls likely to risk their happiness on the forlorn hope of marrying and reforming a captivating rake,) owing to the profane expressions, inconceivably coarse language, and revolting scenes and descriptions by which its pages are disfigured.

Surprised by the hostility of the reviews, Anne wrote a preface to the second edition of *The Tenant*, in which she defended her reasons for writing the book:

> I wished to tell the truth, for truth always conveys its own moral to those who are able to receive it. But as the priceless treasure too frequently hides at the bottom of a well, it needs some courage to dive for it … when we have to do with vice and vicious characters, I maintain it is better to depict them as they really are than as they would wish to appear … If there were less of this delicate concealing of facts … there would be less sin and misery to the young of both sexes who are left to wring their bitter knowledge from experience.

SHIRLEY

I took great pains with SHIRLEY *… but great part of it was written under the shadow of impending calamity, and the last volume I cannot deny was composed in the eager, restless endeavour to combat mental sufferings that were scarcely tolerable.*

CHARLOTTE BRONTË, letter to James Taylor, 1850

Shirley, published in 1849 under Charlotte's Brontë's pseudonym Currer Bell, was the second of her novels to appear in print. Charlotte began writing it early in 1848 but her progress was dogged by ill health: Branwell, Emily and Anne all died during the period of the novel's composition. She had almost completed the second volume of the novel when Branwell died suddenly in September 1848. Following the shock of his death, Charlotte suffered bouts of illness, but as her own health improved, that of her sisters' declined. Soon after Emily died in December it became clear that Anne was also seriously ill. Charlotte often laid the manuscript aside during Anne's illness, and she keenly felt the loss of Emily's encouragement and critical response to her work. After Anne died in May of the following year, Charlotte returned to her writing, an occupation that took her 'out of dark and desolate reality into an unreal but happier region'. As the work progressed, the main protagonists, Caroline Helstone and Shirley Keeldar, took on some of the characteristics of her dead sisters and, in *The Life of Charlotte Brontë*, Elizabeth Gaskell claimed that Shirley became Charlotte's representation of Emily, or

'what Emily Brontë would have been, had she been placed in health and prosperity'.

The final volume of the novel was begun shortly after Anne's death, and by 29 August Charlotte was able to announce to her publishers that the book was completed. Smith, Elder & Co. published *Shirley* in three volumes on 26 October 1849.

In *Shirley*, Caroline Helstone has been brought up by her uncle, the formidable rector of Briarfield, Matthewson Helstone. Her mother fled many years earlier to escape an alcoholic husband, and all that Caroline can learn of her mother is that 'she thinks nothing of you; she never inquires about you.' Caroline is in love with Robert Moore, the tenant of Hollows' Mill, who encounters trouble from his workers when he attempts to bring in new machinery.

Following a quarrel between Mr Helstone and Moore, Caroline is no longer allowed to visit Moore and his sister Hortense. As Caroline determines to prepare herself for a

The ruins of Griffe Mill on the River Worth, below Stanbury, dismantled in 1928.

life without marriage, her uncle introduces her to Shirley Keeldar, a young and fiercely independent woman who has just come into an inheritance and is living near by at Fieldhead. The two women become good friends. During an illness from which Caroline seems unlikely to recover, she is nursed by Shirley's companion, Mrs Pryor, who she learns is really her mother. Her mother's love and care saves Caroline's life.

Shirley is frequently included with a range of novels known as 'condition of England' or 'social problem' novels, typified by works such as Disraeli's *Sybil*, Dickens's

Hard Times and Gaskell's *Mary Barton* and *North and South*. These works showed the social problems created by industrialization. The introduction of labour-saving machinery in the mills meant that many of the mill workers were left unemployed and starving. Large forces of desperate men, known as Luddites, began attacking the mills to destroy newly installed machinery. Charlotte would have heard her father's tales of Luddite violence at Hartshead, and had spent her own schooldays at Mirfield, in the heart of Luddite country. Mrs Gaskell claimed that 'what Charlotte had heard there as a girl came up in her mind when, as a woman, she sought a subject for her next work … She was anxious to write of things she had known and seen; and among the number was the West Yorkshire character, for which any tale laid among the Luddites would afford full scope'.

In *Shirley* Charlotte also presents the arguments for an improvement in the condition of women. Although the novel is set in the years 1811–12, the 'woman question' was very much of the 1840s when Charlotte was writing it. The debate was fuelled by the spectacle of the increasing numbers of middle-class women left unmarried and prevented from any other occupation by convention, and the only profession considered suitable if a woman was forced to work through financial necessity being that of teaching, either in a school or as a private governess.

Although *Shirley* has been seen by critics as less than successful in the fact that it returns to the traditional solution of marriage for its ending, Charlotte herself was well aware that there were no easy answers to the questions she raised.

THE PEOPLE OF SHIRLEY

Shirley was set in Birstall and Gomersal, where Charlotte's friends Ellen Nussey and Mary Taylor lived. Many of the characters were drawn from people Charlotte had known there, although she informed Ellen that she was 'not to suppose any of the characters in *Shirley* intended as literal portraits'. The novel opens with a lively and unflattering representation of three curates at dinner, and despite

LEFT *Oakwell Hall at Birstall (now a museum) was Charlotte's inspiration for Shirley Keeldar's home, Fieldhead.*

RIGHT *So clearly did Mary Taylor visualize Charlotte's description of Briarmains that she was able to inform her that she had 'not seen the matted hall and the painted parlour windows so plain these 5 years'. The windows, still to be seen in the Red House, her old home, are graphically described in the novel: 'Those windows would be seen by daylight to be of brilliantly-stained glass – purple and amber the predominant hues, glittering round a gravely-tinted medallion in the centre of each, representing the suave head of William Shakespeare, and the serene one of John Milton.'*

SHIRLEY

Charlotte's claim that her characters were not to be regarded as 'literal portraits', she admitted to W.S. Williams that 'the curates and their ongoings are merely photographed from the life.' The curates were not the only ones to find themselves portrayed in *Shirley*: a host of other people from the Birstall area recognized themselves and their neighbours in the novel. 'You ask me in one of your letters lately whether I thought I should escape identification in Yorkshire,' Charlotte wrote to her publisher's reader, Mr Williams, adding, 'I am so little known, that I think I shall. Besides the book is far less founded on the Real than perhaps appears.' It seems significant that it was shortly after the publication of this novel that the closely guarded secret of Charlotte's identity as an author was found out.

CRITICAL RECEPTION

A second novel by the author of the wildly successful *Jane Eyre* was received with great excitement. All the reviewers speculated upon the unknown author's sex and identity. 'I wish all reviewers believed "Currer Bell" to be a man; they would be more just to him,' Charlotte wrote to G.H. Lewes, who had produced one of the most wounding pieces of criticism of *Shirley*, adding:

> You will, I know, keep measuring me by some standard of what you deem becoming to my sex; where I am not what you consider graceful you will condemn me … Come what will, I cannot, when I write, think always of myself and of what is elegant and charming in femininity; it is not on those terms, or with such ideas, I ever took my pen in hand: and if it is only on such terms my writing will be tolerated, I shall pass away from the public and trouble it no more.

Critical reception was mixed and a reviewer for the *Atlas* summed up the feelings of many when he wrote: 'It would take a great many Shirleys to put Jane Eyre out of our heads.' The majority of the reviewers appear to have felt that the interest of the story was weakened by being divided among too many characters and they also found the depiction of the male characters in the novel to be unconvincing. The reviewer for the *Daily News* believed that 'The merit of the work lies in the variety, beauty, and truth of its female character. Not one of its men are genuine … They are all as unreal as Madame Tussaud's waxworks.' This view was shared by the reviewer for *Fraser's Magazine*, who commented that the author 'knows women by their brains and hearts, men by their foreheads and chests'. Charlotte felt that the most perceptive of the reviews was by Eugene Forcade, from an article in *Revue des deux mondes*:

> Currer Bell has, however, retained one of the most piquant spices that enlivened his first book and has even increased the dose here and there: the moral freedom, the spirit of insubordination, the impulses of revolt against certain social conventions. The final passage of Shirley is an ironical challenge to those who censured the morality of Jane Eyre: 'the story is told. I think I now see the judicious reader putting on his spectacles to look for the moral. It would be an insult to his sagacity to offer directions. I only say, God speed him in the quest.'

The Red House, Gomersal, which served as Briarmains in SHIRLEY. *The house is now a museum.*

VILLETTE

I am only just returned to a sense of the real world about me, for I have been reading VILLETTE, *a still more wonderful book than* JANE EYRE. *There is something almost preternatural in its power.*

GEORGE ELIOT, letter to Mrs Bray, 15 February 1853

Villette was written after the deaths of Emily and Anne and is a novel born out of Charlotte's loneliness. She struggled to keep writing and it was finally published by Smith, Elder & Co. in January 1853.

Although the book takes its title from the place in which it is set (Villette is based on Brussels), the focus is its heroine, Lucy Snowe. Lucy has come to Villette by a series of chances, having lost her family and suffered hardship earlier in life. She is taken on by Madame Beck, who runs a girls' school. The reader is made acutely aware of Lucy's psychological state as she goes through difficult and lonely situations.

Lucy is strongly attracted to a figure from her past, Dr John, but she comes to realize that he will never love her. While distracted by this, she has started to think with growing warmth of the good qualities of Monsieur Paul Emanuel, the school's English tutor; and in setting aside her feelings for Dr John she realizes that she is in love with Paul Emanuel, and that this feeling is returned. However, the book does not have the conventional happy ending. Charlotte told Mrs Gaskell:

Mr Brontë was anxious that her new tale should end well, as he disliked novels which left a melancholy impression upon the mind; and he requested her to make her hero and heroine (like the heroes and heroines in fairy-tales) 'marry, and live happily ever after.' But the idea of M. Paul Emanuel's death at sea was stamped on her imagination til it assumed the distinct force of reality … All she could do in compliance with her father's wish was to veil the fate in oracular words, as to leave it to the character and discernment of her readers to interpret her meaning.

IMAGINATION AND REALITY

Villette is often described as the most autobiographical of Charlotte Brontë's novels and the scenes and characters have a reality about them that has tempted readers and biographers to make a direct equation between what appears in the books and what happened in Charlotte's own life.

Charlotte's letters indicate that she was happiest with her writing when she could take real people, places or events as a starting point. To her publisher she wrote, 'the weakest character in the book is the one I aimed at making the most beautiful, and if this be the case – the fault lies in its wanting the germ of the *real*, in its being purely imaginary.'

Characteristics of Madame and Monsieur Heger of the Pensionnat Heger, which Charlotte had attended in Brussels, fed into the characters of Madame Beck and Paul Emanuel, and Charlotte's publisher, George Smith, and his mother recognized themselves as the inspiration for Dr John and Mrs Bretton.

Charlotte also used real events to inspire those in the novel. For instance, Lucy Snowe's confession to a Catholic priest was based on her own experience, and descriptions of concerts and exhibitions also contain 'germs of the real' from ones she attended herself in Brussels. It was possibly in Brussels that Charlotte first attended a performance by the great actress Rachel, who later figured as Vashti in *Villette*, and she visited the art galleries, also described in the novel.

An illustration for VILLETTE *by E.M. Wimperis (1872).*

In one of the most memorable scenes in *Villette*, Lucy Snowe has taken a drugged drink and wanders the streets during a fête. Charlotte had never taken opium herself and she described to Mrs Gaskell how she wrote about something beyond her experience: 'She had thought intently on it for many and many a night before falling to sleep, – wondering what it was like, or how it would be, – till at length … she wakened up in the morning with all clear before her, as if she had in reality gone through the experience, and then could describe it, word for word, as it had happened.'

Clearly Charlotte's intense imagination played an important part in her work and to consider her purely as an autobiographical writer is to underestimate her talents.

LEFT *A nineteenth-century engraving of St Gudule in Brussels. In 1843 Charlotte made a 'real' confession to a Catholic priest here, an episode which she later used in* VILLETTE. *In the novel the priest tells Lucy Snowe: 'our faith alone could heal you. Protestantism is altogether too dry, cold, prosaic for you', and invited her to come back. Neither Lucy nor her creator was tempted to risk a return visit.*

ABOVE *The Pensionnat Heger in Brussels, where Charlotte was both pupil and teacher in 1842–3.*

RIGHT *An illustration to* VILLETTE *by Edmund Dulac, 1905.*

CRITICAL RECEPTION

Although not the most popular of Charlotte Brontë's novels, *Villette* is the most critically acclaimed. Unlike her previous works, *Villette* was not condemned for its immorality and 'coarseness' of language, although some critics regretted the 'bitterness' expressed in the novel. Some of the adverse criticism came from those who had known Charlotte personally. 'Why is *Villette* disagreeable?' wrote Matthew Arnold. 'Because the writer's mind contains nothing but hunger, rebellion and rage, and therefore that is all she can, in fact put into her book. No fine writing can hide this thoroughly, and it will be fatal to her in the long run.' The formidable writer and social reformer Harriet Martineau, whom Charlotte had met in London, objected to Charlotte's handling of love, causing a rift in their friendship that was never healed.

Most of the critics recognized the extraordinary originality of *Villette*. 'This book would have made her famous, had she not been so already,' wrote one reviewer. While acknowledging that 'the vast majority of novel readers are certainly more moved by an exciting tale than by any amount of ability in the telling of it,' the reviewer for the *Critic* considered that the author of *Jane Eyre* and *Villette* had 'made popularity by a plot', but maintained her fame 'by good writing'.

THE PROFESSOR

I said to myself that my hero should work his way through life as I had seen real living men work theirs – that he should never get a shilling he had not earned – that no sudden turns should lift him in a moment to wealth and high station – that whatever small competency he might gain should be won by the sweat of his brow.

CHARLOTTE BRONTË, preface to *The Professor*, 1850

When Charlotte completed *The Professor*, her first work written with a view to publication, in April 1846, her insistence on adhering to the 'plain and homely' meant that her novel lacked the thrilling excitement suited to the circulating libraries, and it was rejected by all the publishers to whom she submitted it. Although Smith, Elder & Co. acknowledged its promise, *The Professor* only saw the light of day two years after Charlotte's death, when her husband edited the work for publication and Smith, Elder & Co. published it in a two-volume set in 1857.

The experience of studying in Brussels was of great importance in Charlotte's life and work, and two of her four novels draw directly on that experience. While there, her feelings for Monsieur Heger had developed into an obsession. Her passionate attachment to her 'master', in marked contrast to her contempt for the rest of the school, did not go unnoticed by Madame Heger. She curtailed contact between Charlotte and her husband, and Charlotte's increasing sense of isolation drove her to leave Brussels. Back in Haworth, she wrote to Heger and when he ceased to reply, she suspected his wife of intercepting her letters. The relationship became a major theme in both her Belgian novels. *The Professor* has suffered from being seen as merely an earlier version of her last novel, *Villette*, but although they share a setting, the two books are very different in tone.

In this novel Charlotte makes the references to Brussels explicit: the names of streets and buildings are not fictionalized. As in her Angrian tales, Charlotte adopted a male narrator, William Crimsworth, who leaves England for Brussels to escape working for his sadistic elder brother. He secures work in Monsieur Pelet's boys' school and also teaches at the adjoining girls' school. He is fascinated at first, then repelled, by the head of this school, Zoraide Reuter, and falls in love with one of her teachers, Frances Henri. Zoraide intervenes and succeeds in separating the couple for a time. They later meet and marry, and run a successful school together.

An illustration to THE PROFESSOR by Edmund Dulac, 1905.

THE PROFESSOR

La Mort
de
Napoléon.

traiter

Comment doit on envisager ce sujet ? avec (grande) pompe (de paroles) ou avec simplicité ? C'est selon l'idée qu'on a de Napoléon ou plutôt l'idée qu'on est capable d'en avoir ? Les grands orateurs et les grands écrivains, qui se connaissent en politique, Ceux dont ayant l'esprit en quelque sorte au niveau de celui de Napoléon, comprendre et apprécier ses actes militaires et législatifs, célèbrent sa mort en périodes solennelles et pompeuses qui caractérisent l'oraison funèbre ; mais le simple

CRITICAL RECEPTION

The posthumous publication of *The Professor* in 1857 was largely overshadowed by Mrs Gaskell's gripping biography of its author. 'That the work before us will be read and discussed by all who have read the *Life of Charlotte Brontë* is certain enough,' conceded one of the novel's reviewers, but he predicted that 'the interest excited will be rather curious than deep, and the impression left on the reader one of pain and incompleteness ... On the whole, this tale bears to Currer Bell's later works the relation which a pre-Shakespearian story does to the drama, –– it is curious to an artist or psychologist.'

The Professor, Charlotte felt, was 'deficient in incident and in general attractiveness; yet the middle and latter portions of the work, all that relates to Brussels, the Belgian school, &c. is as good as I can write; it contains more pith, more substance, more reality, in my judgement, than much of *Jane Eyre*.'

OPPOSITE *The Brontë family were fascinated by the military leaders of their recent past. Wellington, Nelson and Napoleon were all the subject of the family's poetry and prose. Charlotte's fascination with the great military leaders is apparent in this essay she wrote during her time in Brussels.*

LEFT *Charlotte and Emily travelled to Brussels with their father, their friend Mary Taylor and her brother Joe. They were able to spend a few days sightseeing in London and then took a boat to Ostend and a public stagecoach to Brussels. During the journey Mr Brontë made use of this little notebook in which he had written down French phrases he thought might be useful. Sharing his children's enthusiasm for Wellington, he made a special visit to Waterloo, scene of the Duke's great victory.*

THE
BRONTËS
AND THEIR
BACKGROUND

LEFT *'Right before the traveller ... rises Haworth village; he can see it for two miles before he arrives, for it is situated on the side of a pretty steep hill, with a background of dun and purple moors, rising and sweeping away.'* Mrs Gaskell, THE LIFE OF CHARLOTTE BRONTË (1857).

ABOVE *Haworth seen from the nearby village of Oakworth.*

109

THE HAWORTH CONTEXT

*Such a life as Miss B's I never heard of before Lady KS described her home to me
as in a village of a few grey stone houses perched up on the north side of a bleak moor –
looking over sweeps of bleak moors.*

ELIZABETH GASKELL, letter to a friend, 1850

Mrs Gaskell's picture of Haworth had been formed before she ever set foot in the village. On the occasion of her first visit to the Parsonage in 1853, Charlotte had warned her that once she left her comfortable home in Manchester, she must set out 'in the spirit which might sustain you … on a brief trip to the back woods of America'.

The fact that Mrs Gaskell was in the unique position of having known Charlotte and visited her at Haworth makes her *Life of Charlotte Brontë* fascinating to read, but it is important not to lose sight of the fact that she was primarily a novelist. The image of Charlotte Brontë she wished to convey influenced not only her depiction of those closest to Charlotte but also her presentation of Haworth. When Mrs Gaskell started work on the *Life* shortly after Charlotte's death in 1855, she set out with the intention of making her readers 'honour the woman as much as they have admired the writer', for although Charlotte's novels were sensationally popular, the works of all three sisters had been condemned for their brutality and 'coarseness'. Her intention of defending Charlotte's reputation against such charges dictated Mrs Gaskell's approach to her subject, and she believed that any coarseness in Charlotte's work could

be excused as the inevitable consequence of her peculiar upbringing and surroundings. In the *Life* she devoted an entire chapter to Haworth, explaining:

> For a right understanding of the life of my dear friend, Charlotte Brontë, it appears to me more necessary in her case than in most others, that the reader should be made acquainted with the peculiar forms of population and society amidst which her earliest years were passed, and from which both her own and her sisters' first impressions of human life must have been received.

During her visit to Haworth, Mrs Gaskell accompanied Charlotte in walks out on to the moors. Charlotte pointed out to her gloomy old houses and told her 'such wild tales of the ungovernable families who lived or had lived therein that Wuthering Heights even seemed tame comparatively'.

Besides these accounts of Haworth and its wild inhabitants, Mrs Gaskell added further colour to her picture of the village derived from Newton's *Life of William Grimshaw*. Grimshaw was the famous leader of the eighteenth-century Evangelical Revival who had lived in Haworth and found the inhabitants to be 'ignorant, brutish

and wicked' when he came among them. Mrs Gaskell's picture suggests that little had changed in the years since.

In fact, Haworth was a busy industrial township. The village earned its living at worsted production, in which over a third of the population were employed in some capacity. By 1850 there were three worsted and spinning mills in Haworth, employing men, women and children. The principal cottage industry was wool combing, for the closure of combing shops by employers increasingly led to the combers being forced to carry out their work in their own homes. The work involved iron stoves being kept alight day and night in unventilated rooms in order to maintain the correct temperature for heating the combs, and contributed to the poor state of health in Haworth.

ABOVE *No one knows for certain when Top Withens was built, but it is reputed to date from the sixteenth century. Throughout the nineteenth century it was occupied by members of the Sunderland family, some of whom are buried in Haworth churchyard. The last recorded occupant was Ernest Roddy, a poultry farmer, in 1926. The main room, raftered and with a stone fireplace, was entered through a small porch. Beyond this there was a smaller room, and a door leading into a narrow vaulted cellar. There were bedrooms above, and a small attic running the length of the house. In an article published in 1893, Harwood Brierley described the interior as 'blue-washed', with rows of oatcakes 'stretched across the dark ceiling'. A bright fire glowed in the grate and the furniture consisted of high-backed chairs and 'a curious chest of dark wood fitted into an angle of the walls'.*

RIGHT *Old Fold Hall dates from the early seventeenth century and is one of the oldest surviving buildings in Haworth. A tablet above the door records the fact that in 1724 the house was purchased and re-fronted by Timothy Horsfall.*

LEFT *A plan of Haworth, surveyed by J.O. Brierly for the newly established Haworth Local Board of Health, 1853.*

RIGHT *Main Street in the late 1870s. The shop in the foreground is that of James Ogden, a linen draper. The white cottages, long since demolished, were occupied by James Whitham, a carrier, and Simeon Townend, a cabinet-maker.*

FAR RIGHT *Ebor Mill, the most complete surviving mill in Haworth.*

FAR RIGHT BELOW *Haworth Old Church, where Patrick Brontë was Perpetual Curate from 1820 until his death in 1861. With the exception of the tower, the building was demolished in 1879 and rebuilt on the same site.*

Many men were employed in the quarrying of stone in the now disued Penistone quarries, and the moors are dotted with the remains of old farmhouses where the hardy inhabitants once eked out a living from subsistence farming. Gradually the local water authority bought up the old farms. Fearing sewage seepage to the reservoirs constructed in the late nineteenth and early twentieth centuries, it left the farms to fall into decay.

The census records 3,518 people living in the township of Haworth in 1851, a figure that includes the Main Street area and outlying farms. Although in the 1850s there were over a thousand Irish immigrants living in the nearby town of Keighley, there were only six recorded in Haworth at that time, and two of these were Patrick Brontë and his curate, Arthur Bell Nicholls.

Haworth chiefly consists of the Main Street, a string of eighteenth- and early nineteenth-century stone cottages cut into the steep Pennine hillside. Main Street is cobbled with stone setts placed endways, which Mrs Gaskell tells us were intended 'to give a better hold to the horses' feet; even with this help, they seem to be in constant danger of slipping backwards.' The side streets were little more than dirt tracks. One of these is Lodge Street, known as Newell Hill in the Brontës' time, where the meetings of the Three Graces Masonic Lodge came to be held. Ginnels and alleyways led to the poorer cottages, since demolished, which were crowded together at the top of the Main Street.

Standing at the top of Main Street and visible for miles around is the Church of St Michael and All Angels, where Patrick Brontë officiated for over forty years. Church and

chapel were central to religious life and also provided much of the community's social life. Haworth has a history of religious Non-conformity and a number of Methodist and Baptist chapels remain. The oldest of these was built by a group of Baptists in 1824, on the village green near the Old Hall. The first Minister of Hall Green Chapel was Moses Saunders, who regularly clashed with Mr Brontë over theological issues. The land surrounding the chapel was used as a burial ground. One of the first plots was that bought by seventeen-year-old Faithy Sutcliffe, who died the following year and became the first person to be buried there. Towards the end of the century the burial ground was fast filling up, and the registers contain notes indicating where there was 'Room for one more' and 'Room for one infant'. Approximately six hundred people are buried here.

Haworth had already attracted fame a century before Mr Brontë's arrival under the ministry of William Grimshaw, whose biographer, John Newton, claimed that

LEFT *Lodge Street, leading off Main Street, takes its name from the fact that meetings of the Masonic Lodge of the Three Graces, to which Branwell was initiated in 1836, took place here. The house facing was the home of William Wood, joiner and cabinet maker. The blocked-up doorway formerly led to his workshop on the second floor.*

RIGHT *The interior of Hall Green Baptist Chapel in Haworth, looking much as it would have done when built in 1824.*

the 'name of Haworth, would scarcely be known at a distance, were it not connected with the name of Grimshaw.' Colourful tales abound of him haranguing sinners and driving his parishioners from public house to church, brandishing a horsewhip. His sudden death in 1763 robbed the Evangelicals of a leading light.

The exact date of the foundation of Haworth church is not known. It is often claimed that the church dates from ancient times, although the first reliable reference to a church at Haworth occurs in 1317. The historian Steven Wood believes that a new church was built in 1488 and extended in 1600. When Grimshaw came to Haworth in 1742, his preaching attracted such huge congregations that it became necessary to enlarge the church. The work was completed in 1755, and this church, with its three-decker pulpit and oak box pews, was essentially the church the Brontës knew.

By the 1870s the building had fallen into a poor state , and it became clear that many costly repairs were required.

At this point Michael Merrall, a mill owner and one of the biggest employers in Haworth, stepped in and offered £5,000 towards the cost of a new building. Although the building may not have been considered important in architectural terms – Mrs Gaskell described the interior as 'common-place': 'neither old enough nor modern enough to compel notice' – its association with Grimshaw and the Brontës meant that there was a great deal of opposition to its proposed demolition, much of it from outside the village. Various alternatives were rejected, and with the exception of the tower, the old church was demolished in 1879 and rebuilt on the same site. The new building, described by one commentator as 'ready-made Gothic', was consecrated in 1881.

Most of Haworth's public houses are clustered at the top of the Main Street within a stone's throw of the church. In 1848 there were five public houses in Haworth. The Black Bull, famed for its association with Branwell Brontë, appears in records for 1744 and is probably the oldest. In 1847 the landlord is recorded as Enoch Thomas, whose brother William founded the firm of wine and spirit merchants close by. Both men were Masons and associates of Branwell.

A narrow lane at the top of Main Street, climbing past the church and the Sunday school, leads to the Parsonage – virtually the last house in Haworth before the open moors. This is the landscape usually associated with the Brontës, described so hauntingly by Charlotte:

> when I go out there alone everything reminds me of the times when others were with me, and then the moors seem a wilderness, featureless, solitary, saddening. My sister Emily had a particular love for them, and there is not a knoll of heather, not a branch of fern, not a young bilberry leaf, not a fluttering lark or linnet, but reminds me of her. The distant prospects were Anne's delight, and when I look round she is in the blue tints, the pale mists, the waves and shadows of the horizon.

Elizabeth Gaskell's biography put the 'wild, strange facts' of the Brontës' lives before the reading public, and the combination of their own life histories, the passionate intensity of their writing and the harsh beauty of their moorland home proved to be a potent mix. The Brontë myth was born, and people from all over the world beat a path to Haworth, often drawn by the sad story of the Brontës' lives as much as the power of their writing.

THE HAWORTH CONTEXT

LEFT *Hall Green Chapel is the oldest surviving place of worship in Haworth.*

RIGHT ABOVE *The interior of Haworth Old Church, c.1870, with the Brontë memorial tablet.*

RIGHT BELOW *Elizabeth Gaskell claimed that Branwell Brontë's conversational skills earned him 'the undesirable distinction of having his company recommended by the landlord of the Black Bull to any chance traveller who might happen to feel solitary or dull over his liquor'. Despite the fact that alcoholism contributed to Branwell's death at the age of thirty-one, it was estimated that consumption of beer and spirits in Haworth was very much below average.*

LIFE AND DEATH IN HAWORTH

This World's a City, full of crooked streets.
Death is the Market place, Where all men meets.
If life was Merchandise that men could buy,
The rich would live, the Poor must always die.

GRAVESTONE INSCRIPTION, Haworth churchyard

In 1850, the General Board of Health commissioned B.H. Babbage to report on Haworth's water supply and sanitary provision. Inured to dirt and disease, he was still shocked by the conditions he found. He concluded that despite Haworth's hilltop setting and open aspect, the township's average life expectancy of 25.8 years corresponded with that of some of the unhealthiest districts of London.

It is difficult not to be moved by the many memorials to children in Haworth churchyard:

IN
Memory of Bernard Hartley
of Ebor, who died Septr 20th
1841, Aged 41 Years.
ALSO of Eleven Children of
His who all died Young
ALSO of BETTY their Daughter
Who died Feby 7th 1842
Aged 14 Years.

IN MEMORY OF
Mark, Son of George and Rebecca
Binns of Haworth, who died June
20th 1824, Aged one Year.
ALSO of Joseph their Son who
died July 29th 1824, Aged 2 Years.
Under this Stone there lies as you may see
Two lovely Babes, they once was dear to me.
Dearer to God who took them hence away
With whom I leave them till the final day.
ALSO of SARAH & ELIZABETH
their daughters
who died 25th Dec 1833
Aged 1 and 2 Years.
Also of ROBERT, their Son
Who died 25th May 1835
Aged 5 Years.

Babbage estimated that over 41 per cent of the children in Haworth died before reaching the age of six. In his report he went on to say:

> It is lamentable to think that so large an amount of infantile mortality should have been taking place year after year, unknown and unheeded … Nor is it this large proportion of deaths alone which are to be deplored, but where this amount of infantile mortality prevails, who shall picture the mother's anxious care for her drooping offspring, the father's hard tasked labour to provide his family with the needful food and medicines, and the amount of pain and sorrow and disease, which the surviving children have to struggle through before they get beyond this fatal epoch, and acquire an average chance of life.

Many of the causes of death in Haworth were recorded as 'unknown' and Babbage estimated that 21.7 per cent of the population died without receiving any medical attention. Emily Brontë falls into this category. In registering her death Dr Wheelhouse claimed to have been 'in attendance' and certified that she had died from 'Consumption', yet it is known that she refused to see a doctor and he never actually attended her until she was dead. This lack of 'any person to certify the cause of death', Babbage considered, 'affords very great facility for the concealment of crime, ranging from murder in its naked form, through the various finely shaded gradations of ill-treatment, starvation, and neglect'. The Sagar case illustrates his concerns. John Sagar was accused of poisoning his wife, and at his trial at York Assizes in 1858, it was suggested that not all his eight children, buried in a single grave at Haworth, died from natural causes. Though the case collapsed (much of the evidence was ruled inadmissible), it shows what might have been taking place under the very noses of people in Haworth.

In the burial registers for Haworth parish the period 1788 to 1812 is of particular interest because causes of death have been included, and these are unlikely to have changed during the Brontë period. By far the most common cause of death is attributed to 'Decline', a term used to describe a variety of wasting diseases including tuberculosis. Other killers include: 'Fever', 'Scarlet Fever', 'Fits', 'Cancer', 'Inflamation', 'Rheumatick Feaver', 'Croup', 'Measles',

LEFT *A ginnel which once linked Main Street with the Brandy Row area, also known as Gauger's Croft or Piccadilly, where Haworth's working poor lived in damp, overcrowded cottages.*

OPPOSITE *Brandy Row, which took its name from the fact that it was approached through a courtyard adjoining the premises of a wine and spirits merchant. It was demolished around 1970.*

'Dropsy' and 'Childbirth'. There were deaths caused by falls from horses and accidents in the local quarries and drownings (mainly children), and there was one 'poor man who hanged himself'. Although this is the only suicide recorded as such, there were others. Thomas Lister, a cotton spinner of Hollings Mill near Stanbury, hanged himself in 1842 following a depression in trade. The Reverend Thomas Brooksbank Charnock hanged himself in 1847. As suicides, both these men could have been refused a church burial, but not only were they buried in the churchyard, but Patrick Brontë conducted their funerals himself rather than delegating this duty to his curate.

The sanitary state of the township was appalling. The Brontës fared slightly better than many of their neighbours, having their own two-seater privy in their back yard, but in some instances one privy was shared by the inhabitants of twenty-four overcrowded houses. Babbage reported:

> Whilst the number of privies is so limited as to be injurious to health, their situation in many instances, is not less repugnant to all ideas of decency. Two of the privies used, by a dozen families each, are in the public street, not only within view of the houses, but exposed to the gaze of passers by, whilst a third, as though even such a situation were too private, is perched upon an eminence, commanding the whole length of the main street. The cesspit of this privy lies below it, and opens by a small door into the main street; occasionally this door is burst open by the super-incumbent weight of night-soil and ashes, and they overflow into the public street, and at all times a disgusting effluvium escapes through this door into the street. Within two yards of this cesspit-door there is a tap for the supply of water to the neighbouring houses.

Health improvements came about very slowly in the years after the Babbage report, and the area known in the nineteenth century as Brandy Row, where many of the poorer people lived, was one of the last to benefit. Over a hundred years later, a report published by the Civic Trust condemned many of these houses as 'technically unfit' and found that one block had 'only one exterior lavatory for three houses'.

There was no mains sewerage system in Haworth, and what Babbage euphemistically terms 'night soil' was emptied into heaps of household refuse and left to be carted away by farmers. Noxious matter ran in an open channel down the Main Street, making life particularly unpleasant

to around 150 households, though in summer the supply dwindled to such an extent that to be sure of getting enough water for Monday's washing, people sometimes had to set off as early as two o'clock in the morning. Babbage was informed that at this time of year the water was often so green and putrid that cattle refused to drink it.

One enterprising Haworth inhabitant rented Sowden's Spring and built a small cistern from which water was supplied, by means of lead pipes, to between thirty and forty homes in the village. Tragically, while people in Haworth continued to sicken and die, the implementation of Babbage's recommendations was delayed by several of Patrick Brontë's wealthier parishioners who already had access to this private water supply and objected to paying an increased rate to benefit the less well served. A small reservoir was built in 1858, although this soon proved inadequate, and it was not until the 1890s that an agreement

for the occupants of the twenty-five cellar dwellings in Haworth, whose homes were occasionally flooded. Elizabeth Gaskell notes that, not surprisingly, the Brontës preferred to take their walks 'out towards the heathery moors … than towards the long descending village street'.

There was clearly a desperate need for not only the installation of an effective sewerage system but also the provision of an adequate water supply. The township was served by eleven pumps (only nine of which were in use) and two wells. A further five private wells provided water for individual households, including the Parsonage. Mr Brontë noted in his account book that in 1847 the Parsonage well was cleared of eight decomposing tin cans, which had tinged the water yellow. To obtain purer water for drinking or cooking, the inhabitants of one household were prepared to walk to Spring Head, a quarter of a mile away at the bottom of a steep hill. The Head Well supplied water

ABOVE *Haworth Old Church and churchyard, c.1861. With the exception of the tower, the building was demolished in 1879 and rebuilt on the same site. The Old Church had a double-gabled roof, the outline of which can still be seen on the tower.*

RIGHT *In his 1850 report, Babbage condemned the practice of covering graves with large flat stones, which prevented the access of air to the ground and the growth of plants that would assist decomposition. The trees we see in the churchyard today were planted in 1864.*

LIFE AND DEATH IN HAWORTH

was made to have water supplied from Keighley's reservoirs. For much of the nineteenth century the available water was contaminated by the stinking midden heaps and privies that overflowed into the streets and by deadly seepage from the overcrowded churchyard above the village.

At the very start of his career in Haworth Patrick Brontë wrote a letter to the Archbishop of York stressing the urgent need to extend the churchyard, although it was four years before his request was dealt with. Babbage estimated that the 1,344 burials that had taken place in the previous ten years alone must have virtually filled the entire churchyard. He recommended that the churchyard be closed immediately, and stressed the dangers of siting a badly drained graveyard in close proximity to housing:

A most striking example of the state of the water draining from a churchyard is to be found at Castleford, where an addition to the churchyard was made by enclosing a small piece of ground, through which ran a covered drain, leading into the ditch which bounded the rector's garden. There was evidence of the actual communication between this drain and the graves. The smell arising at the mouth of the open part of this ditch, was one of the most nauseous and fetid nature which I ever came across … I consider, then the speedy carrying away in covered channels of the water charged with this most dangerous and most subtle matter, to be one of the most efficacious means of diminishing the evils, which there can be no doubt always take place from the vicinity of burial-grounds to inhabited places.

Haworth churchyard would have made an appropriately gloomy resting place for the Brontës, and many visitors to the area are disappointed on learning that they are in fact buried inside the church. One of these visitors was the poet Matthew Arnold, who visited Haworth in 1853. When he came to write his elegy 'Haworth Churchyard, April, 1855' on the death of Charlotte, he imaginatively placed Charlotte and her siblings 'In a churchyard high mid the moors' and was not pleased to learn of his mistake. In a letter to Mrs Gaskell he wrote: 'I am almost sorry you told me about the place of their burial. It really seems to me to put the finishing touch to the strange cross-grained character of the fortunes of that ill-fated family that they should even be placed after death in the wrong, uncongenial spot.'

Babbage noted that within the past twenty years there had been 'about 12' burials in the vaults beneath the church. This figure included members of the Brontë family, for apart from Anne, who died and was buried at Scarborough, they were all laid to rest in a family vault beneath the floor of the chancel. Burial inside the church was a practice 'to which an entire stop should be put' as far as Babbage was concerned. When Patrick Brontë died in 1861, despite an Order in Council reserving his right to be buried in the church, permission had to be sought from the Secretary of State before he could be interred with his family. This was granted on condition that his coffin was embedded in a layer of powdered charcoal and separately entombed in brick or stone. During the rebuilding of the church in 1879–81 it was feared that six of the graves beneath the floor might have to be disturbed, and it has been suggested that the Brontë vault was one of these. The faculty authorizing the demolition of the church provides details of the graves under possible threat but makes no mention of the Brontë vault. A son of the Reverend John Wade, the incumbent of

Haworth at that time, claimed that 'The Brontë grave was in no way interfered with, and the remains were left where they were placed at their funerals … Over their grave, as over the others, was laid a thick layer of concrete … upon which the present edifice stands.'

William Wood, the aptly named Haworth joiner, made not only some of the Parsonage furniture but also the Brontë coffins. His account books recording details of some of these were still around in 1930, when they were partially transcribed:

Nov. 2, 1842 Miss Bramwell coffen £5-12-6 [Miss Branwell had died on 29 October and was buried on 3 November]

Patrack Bramwell Bronty aged 30 years Died Septr: 24 – A.D 1848

A.D. 1848 in graven. Black cloth 15/-, mettle tire 15/- To flanell & riben 10/3. Coffen & scroud making £1-5.
£3-15

In Memory
OF
EMILY JANE BRONTE,
WHO DIED
DECEMBER XIX, M DCCCXLVIII,
AGED TWENTY-NINE YEARS.

Joseph Fox, Confectioner.

And finally:

> Emlea Jane Bronty. Died Dec 19th 1848 in the 30 year of hir Age. Coffen 5ft 7" long 16" broad.

William Wood found a steady trade in making coffins in Haworth. Of the many he produced, he believed that Emily's was the narrowest he had ever made for an adult. We tend to think of the Brontë sisters as frail, sickly women, but in mid-nineteenth-century Haworth their early deaths would have been unremarkable.

William Wood, along with many of the Brontës' former friends, servants and neighbours, was eventually laid to rest in the churchyard at Haworth. Here the old Haworth names of Binns, Feather, Greenwood, Hartley, Heaton and Holmes abound. A wander around the churchyard can tell you quite a lot about the people who once lived and died here, and one thing we can be sure of: although the Brontës suffered, they did not suffer alone.

LEFT *Funeral card for Emily Jane Brontë, whose burial took place on Friday 22 December 1848. Winifred Gerin describes how 'On this occasion, the order of their going was remembered by generations of the villagers; behind the coffin walked Mr Brontë with Keeper, who at Mr Brontë's wish stayed at the head of the little procession and entered the family box-pew with them, where he remained throughout the service. After them walked Charlotte and Anne, and behind them Tabby, an old woman of seventy-eight, and Martha.'*

RIGHT *A cobbled yard and outbuildings off West Lane.*

HAWORTH PARSONAGE

*It was a low stone house, which occupied one corner of the graveyard. A field
(in the deeds it is called a croft) had evidently been set apart, and the founders of the
church had said 'in three quarters of it we will inter the dead and in that other
fourth we will bury the living' ... of all the sad, heart-broken dwellings I have passed,
this was the saddest.*

FRANK PEEL, *History of the Spen Valley*, 1893

ABOVE *Haworth Church and Parsonage,
c.1860. Mrs Gaskell, visiting in 1853, recalled
how 'on autumnal or winter nights, the four
winds of heaven seemed to meet and rage
together, tearing round the house as if they
were wild beasts trying to find an entrance.'*

RIGHT *A view of Church Street, looking
towards the Brontë Parsonage Museum,
with the church Sunday school on the right.*

surrounds the house on two sides. Haworth Parsonage has become redolent of the Brontës' short sad lives, and it often comes as a surprise to visitors to find that, unlike the gloomy haunted house of Brontë mythology, the Parsonage is attractive and comfortable within.

The Parsonage, or Glebe House as it was originally known, was built in 1778–9 of the local millstone grit. The first occupant was the Reverend John Richardson, and following his death in 1791, the Parsonage became the home of James Charnock. Little is known about Charnock's twenty-eight years of residency and it is not even known for certain that he actually occupied the house for all the period of his incumbency.

Commenting on his new position, Patrick Brontë wrote: 'My salary is not large; it is only about £200 a year. I have a good house, which is mine also, and is rent-free.' The Parsonage, along with land at Stanbury that paid the incumbent's salary, was vested in the hands of trustees. If Mr Brontë's health failed, the family stood to lose both home and income. Mrs Brontë received a small annuity, but this came to an end when she died within eighteen months of the family's arrival at Haworth. In the event, Patrick Brontë was to outlive all his family.

Mrs Gaskell was the only Brontë biographer to have visited the Parsonage during the lifetimes of Charlotte and Patrick Brontë. She paid her first visit in 1853 when, apart from the servants, they lived there alone. In a letter to a friend, she wrote:

Haworth Parsonage was the home of the Brontë family for over forty years, and it was here that the famous Brontë novels were written. The family moved into the house in 1820, following Patrick Brontë's appointment as Perpetual Curate. 'One wonders', reflected Mrs Gaskell, 'how the bleak aspect of her new home – the low, oblong stone parsonage, high up, yet with a higher backdrop of sweeping moors – struck on the gentle, delicate wife whose health was even then failing.'

To the family, it would simply have offered more space than their previous home, and it was undoubtedly one of the better houses in the village. The elegant Georgian façade stands in contrast to the semi-wild churchyard that

I don't know that I ever saw a spot more exquisitely clean … Everything fits into, and is in harmony with, the idea of a country parsonage, possessed by people of very moderate means. Everything about the place tells of the most dainty order, the most exquisite cleanliness. The door-steps are spotless; the small old-fashioned window-panes glitter like looking-glass. Inside and outside of that house cleanliness goes up into its essence, purity.

Following the publication of Mrs Gaskell's *Life of Charlotte Brontë* in 1857, visitors from all over the world made the pilgrimage to Haworth. Mr Brontë was eighty years of age by this time, but would often grant interviews to admirers of his daughters' works. Following his death, the Parsonage served as home to his successors: John Wade (1861–98), T.W. Storey (1898–1919), G.A. Elson (1919–25) and J.C. Hirst (1925–8). They were all, understandably, less tolerant of these uninvited 'gazers'.

The Parsonage is set above the village and separated from it by the church and a square plot of garden – given over to rough grass and a few stunted bushes in the Brontës' time. Ellen Nussey recalled how, on stepping out from the garden gate, you looked across to the stonemason's chipping shed, 'piled with slabs ready for use', and that the daily routine of the Brontës' lives at Haworth was accompanied by the incessant 'chip, chip, of the recording chisel as it graved the In Memoriams of the departed.'

RIGHT *Mr Brontë spent much of his time in his study, where he was described in old age as 'sitting in a plain, uncushioned chair, upright as a soldier' before the fire.*

FAR RIGHT *The flagged entrance hall and stone stairs at the Parsonage survive from the Brontës' time. Charlotte probably added the arch in 1850 when she enlarged the dining room.*

The back yard contained a peat store and the two-seater privy, with seats for adults and children. Here also was a well, fed by moorland springs, and in the Brontës' time, the moor crept almost to the back door of the Parsonage.

A large wash kitchen, built on the back of the house by Mr Brontë, was demolished in the 1870s before the construction of large side and rear extensions to the house. Otherwise the Parsonage is much as the Brontës would have known it. The front door leads into the flagged entrance hall, 'always beautifully clean as everything about the house was', Ellen Nussey recalled. Flagstone floors extended to all the ground-floor rooms, and when Ellen first visited in 1833, there was 'not much carpet anywhere except in the sitting room, and on the centre of the study floor'. The stone floors and exposed situation make the Parsonage a cold house. A mixture of coal and peat would have been burnt for heat, and Mrs Gaskell recalled how fires burning in the grates made a 'pretty warm dancing light all over the house'.

The room to the right of the entrance hall was Mr Brontë's study. Despite the room's sparse furnishings, it was rich in books and prints. It housed Mr Brontë's well-used library, and on the walls hung black-and-white engravings of John Martin's apocalyptic paintings *The Plains of Heaven* and *The Last Judgement*. The Brontës' imaginations were stirred by Martin's fantastic visions, and passages from their early writings derive from descriptions of these marvellous scenes. Against the wall was a cottage piano, which Emily played with 'brilliancy'.

Across the hall is the dining room, where the Brontë children studied and played, exploring their own imaginary worlds, writing and illustrating their tiny hand-made books. As young adults, the sisters developed a nightly ritual of walking round the dining-room table, discussing their writing. After the deaths of Emily and Anne, Martha Brown, the family servant, described how her heart ached 'to hear Miss Brontë walking, walking on alone'.

The room's simple furnishings include a mahogany table and chairs. Mrs Gaskell observed that Charlotte's sense of order was such that she could not continue a conversation if a chair was out of place. A black horsehair sofa is said to be the one on which Emily died in December 1848.

The austerity of the house had not made itself felt in former days, but after the deaths of her sisters, Charlotte took some pleasure in making the Parsonage more comfortable. The income from her writing allowed her to carry out alterations, and in 1850 she enlarged the dining room and the main bedroom above. Ellen Nussey remembered how 'Mr Brontë's horror of fire forbad curtains to the windows,' but Charlotte began to assert her independence and ordered new curtains for the dining room. Although her father was not pleased, he did not object. When Mrs Gaskell visited the house three years later, she noted that the room had 'evidently been refurbished within the last few years …The prevailing colour of the room is crimson, to make a warm setting for the cold grey landscape without.'

The room behind the dining room was originally 'a sort of flagged store room', which

OPPOSITE *The dining room at Haworth Parsonage, where the sisters did much of their writing, and where, in the evening, they would walk around the table discussing their work.*

LEFT ABOVE *The Brontë sisters were expected to carry out their share of household tasks, and the kitchen features in many of their accounts of daily life at the Parsonage.*

LEFT BELOW *The former store room that Charlotte converted into a study for her husband-to-be, Arthur Bell Nicholls.*

Charlotte converted into a study for her husband, Arthur Bell Nicholls, in 1854. Describing her preparations for the room's conversion, Charlotte wrote: 'Since I came home I have been very busy stitching – the little new room is got into order now and the green and white curtains are up – they look neat and clean enough.'

Behind Mr Brontë's study is the kitchen, the warm hub of the house, where the young Brontës would gather round the fire on winter evenings to listen to Tabby Aykroyd's dark tales of the Yorkshire moors. The sisters were expected to share in the household chores, and Emily in particular was often to be found helping in the kitchen or baking the bread. A visitor to the Parsonage in the late 1850s recalled how 'Every thing was exquisitely neat, and the copper pans shone like gold. It was a snug, warm crooning place … Here Emily Brontë studied German, with her book propped up before her, while she kneaded dough.'

Halfway up the stone staircase stood a long-case clock that Mr Brontë would wind at nine o'clock every night on his way to bed. There are two bedrooms at the back of the house. The first was occupied by the servants; the other was used as a studio by Branwell at one period, but for much of the time served as a bedroom used by different members of the family.

There are three rooms at the front of the house. To the right of the landing, over the dining room, is the bedroom in which Mrs Brontë spent the last dreary months of her life, and where she died in 1821. The room was taken over by her elder sister, Aunt Branwell, and after her death in 1842 different members of the family, and the occasional guest, occupied it. Mrs Gaskell slept here in 1853, and found the view from the window 'really beautiful in certain lights, moon-light especially'. When Charlotte married, she and her husband shared the room. It was here that Charlotte died on 31 March 1855, at the age of thirty-eight.

After the death of his wife, Mr Brontë moved into the room across the landing, which he occupied for the rest of his life. In later years, Branwell's addiction to alcohol and laudanum made him a danger both to himself and his family and an early biographer, Mary Robinson, was told how on one occasion Branwell, stupefied by alcohol, set his bed on fire and was rescued by Emily. Whether or not the story is true, fear of such incidents led Mr Brontë to share his room with his son, in order to watch over him. Mrs Gaskell relates how Branwell suffered attacks of delirium tremens, and would sometimes declare that 'either he or his father should be dead before morning'. When morning came, 'young Brontë would saunter out, saying, with a drunkard's incontinence of speech, "the poor old man and I have had a terrible night of it; he does his best – the poor old man! But it's all over with me."' It was in this room that Branwell died at the age of thirty-one, on Sunday 24 September 1848. Having outlived his wife and all his children, Mr Brontë also died here on 7 June 1861.

In the nineteenth century it was common for families to share rooms, and it is difficult to be certain which members of the family slept where as the children grew up and spent time away from home. The tiny room squeezed in between Charlotte's room and her father's is now only 157 centimetres wide, but it was wider before Charlotte's structural alterations to the right-hand wall. In the early days it served as a nursery and was known as 'the children's study'. Later it became Emily's room. Her diary paper of 1845 includes a sketch she made of herself seated here with her portable writing desk on her lap. Her dog Keeper lies near her feet, while another dog is curled on the bed.

When Patrick Brontë's successor, John Wade, took up residence at the Parsonage in 1861, he evidently found the house cramped and inconvenient. Unlike Mr Brontë, he possessed a private income that enabled him to enlarge and improve the Parsonage. In 1878 he outraged many Brontë enthusiasts when he added a large gabled wing to the house in order to create more space for his own growing family. The back kitchen, where the washing and heavier household work were carried out, was demolished to make way for a new kitchen extension, which blocked the mullioned window that had looked out towards the moors in the Brontës' time. The range was removed and the old kitchen became a passageway to Wade's dining room in the new wing. Two extra bedrooms and bathrooms were created above, and the room that had once been Branwell's studio was merged into a staircase to make a way through to the new part of the house. Repairs and alterations were made to the original part, for it appears that despite Charlotte's improvements in the 1850s, the house had fallen into a sad state of neglect. A visitor who arrived in Haworth as Wade's alterations were being carried out was told:

> Mr Brontë disliked to have mechanical work going on there. Only once, from absolute necessity, to keep out bad leakage, he allowed the roof to be mended. The new incumbent does not choose to go into a rotten old house, but they are doing very much more than making merely necessary repairs. They are putting in fireplaces and mantelpieces of marble, and windows of plate glass, a single pane filling the whole sash and weighing thirty pounds.

Nowadays the glazing bars have been replaced, and the house has been restored to its original appearance. Contemporary descriptions and the hand-written catalogue of the sale of the contents of the Parsonage in 1861 following Mr Brontë's death provide valuable information about the way the house was furnished in the Brontës' time,

and today the majority of the rooms are set out in as close an approximation as possible to their appearance in the Brontës' day. Fortunately, thanks to the efforts of the Brontë Society, much of the original furniture has been returned to the Parsonage, and most of the household items on display actually belonged to the family.

OPPOSITE *This mahogany long-case clock, made by Barraclough of Haworth, is believed to have been the one that stood halfway up the stairs, which Mr Brontë would wind on his way to bed.*

ABOVE *The double-vaulted cellar beneath the Parsonage is not usually included in a tour of the museum. It is easy to imagine the Brontë children acting out their plays here.*

THE BRONTËS' SOCIAL CIRCLE

*Mrs Brontë's illness had been sufficient excuse for lack of neighbourliness,
and after her death the bereaved husband had little desire to enter into
any society … the sociable Vicar of Thornton, who had enjoyed the little
tea parties with his wife at Kipping, became a recluse, and his children had
to find their pleasures on the moors, or in the kitchen with the servants …*

MRS ELLIS H. CHADWICK, *In the Footsteps of the Brontës*, 1914

It is popularly believed that the Brontës were extremely isolated in their parsonage home: that they had few friends and little contact with the outside world. This is a view that originated with Charlotte Brontë herself, for she recorded in her *Biographical Notice*: 'Resident in a remote district where education had made little progress, and where, consequently, there was no inducement to seek social intercourse beyond our own domestic circle, we were wholly dependent on ourselves and each other, on books and study for the enjoyments and occupations of life.'

An early biographer of the Brontës, Mrs Chadwick, relates how when the Brontës were invited to a birthday party at the home of one of the church trustees, it was found, 'much to the surprise of their little friends, the Brontë children had no idea of the ordinary games that any village child could play.' Although the Brontës had little contact with children of their own age, they had no need of outside companionship, for they had each other, and developed their own extraordinary games of the imagination.

Losing his wife so soon after the move to Haworth meant that Patrick Brontë looked back to the happier times at Thornton. 'In this place', he confided to a friend of those days, 'I have received civilities, and have I trust, been civil to all, but I have not tried to make any friends, nor have I met with any whose mind, was congenial, with my own.' Not seeking society himself, Mr Brontë did little to foster social contacts for his children. Mrs Gaskell describes the sisters as having grown up 'bereft, in a singular manner, of all such society as would have been natural to their age, sex, and station'. The girls grew up gauche and ill at ease in company, and they were further marked out by their singular, old-fashioned dresses. An English family who attempted to befriend Charlotte and Emily in Brussels described how 'Emily hardly ever muttered more than a monosyllable, and Charlotte was sometimes excited sufficiently to speak eloquently and well – on certain subjects – but, before her tongue was loosed, she had a habit of gradually wheeling round on her chair, so as almost to conceal her face from the person to whom she was speaking.' The visits were clearly a source of more pain than pleasure and came to an abrupt end. While Charlotte wished to please, Emily was indifferent to the impression she made on others.

The Brontës had few intellectual equals in Haworth, a sprawling community in which the majority of the population were employed in combing wool for the factories, with few educational opportunities. One Haworth inhabitant is reported to have said of Mr Brontë that 'he minds his own business, and ne'er troubles himself with ours.' Thus Mr Brontë's unsociability is seen as extending to his parishioners. A life of complete isolation, however, would not have been possible for Mr Brontë or his family. The duties of a clergyman at that time were wide-ranging and encompassed both social welfare and the control of civil order. No effort was spared by Mr Brontë in attempts to improve the lot of the villagers and, as the daughters of a clergyman, the Brontë sisters would have been expected to take an active role in their father's work by visiting the needier residents of the parish and teaching Sunday school classes. Once every year the female Sunday

ABOVE *Branwell's portrait of John Brown, the Haworth sexton and stonemason, who lived in the house adjoining the Sunday school. According to Francis Leyland, it was 'no infrequent circumstance to see … Branwell listening to the coarse jokes of the sexton of Haworth – the noted John Brown – while that functionary was employed in digging the graves so often opened in the churchyard, under the shadow of the Parsonage'.*

school teachers would be invited to tea at the Parsonage. One of these invitations took place while Charlotte's friend Ellen Nussey was staying there. Ellen was rather shocked by these young Haworth women, who were nearly all 'earners of their daily bread at the factories', but who 'manifested none of that deferential respect towards their employers which was the general tone of the well-employed in most other localities'. They showed 'a rough respect to their entertainers, and great good nature also, for on discovering that the Miss Brontës were willing to play games with them but did not know how, they undertook to initiate them.'

Even Branwell Brontë was not exempt from involvement in his father's parish duties. He, like his sisters, was expected to teach in the Sunday school. Unlike his sisters, however, Branwell had no domestic responsibilities, and while his father was occupied with parochial business, Branwell was often 'thrown into chance companionship with the lads of the village'. He appears to have enjoyed a degree of popularity in Haworth that was not shared by his sisters. An American visitor to Haworth in 1861, who wished to discuss the Brontë sisters with those who had actually known them, noted that it was 'singular how all these people at once diverge from the girls to Branwell'. It was said of Branwell that 'His personality seemed far clearer to them than that of his father and sisters. He had evidently associated intimately with them, was in and out of their homes, and, unfortunately, hail-fellow-well-met with every ne'er-do-well.'

According to the testimony of many in the village, Branwell was remembered as the most outgoing and sociable member of his family, with a wide circle of friends and acquaintances both around Haworth and further afield. He threw himself into whatever social life Haworth had to offer and ironically, bearing in mind his spectacular decline into alcoholism, he was for a time secretary of the Haworth Temperance Society. Branwell's great friend in Haworth was John Brown, thirteen years his senior and sexton of Haworth church. Brown, whose portrait by Branwell still survives in the Parsonage Museum, was also Worshipful Master of the local Masonic Lodge, to which Branwell was initiated in 1836.

Branwell took full advantage of any opportunities for socializing when away from Haworth, often to the exclusion of his work. When he tried his hand at portraiture in a studio in Bradford in 1838, among those he met at the George Hotel were local poets and historians, the sculptor Joseph Bentley Leyland and painters Wilson Anderson and

Richard Waller. Leyland was a rather glamorous figure who had rejected a promising future in London, choosing instead to remain in Halifax, where he eventually died in the debtors' prison. Later, while working as a railway clerk in Halifax at Luddenden Foot, Branwell was once again lured away from his isolated post by the warmth and conviviality of the local public houses. He never managed to combine business and pleasure successfully. Francis Grundy, the young engineer who met Branwell at this time, was able to view Branwell's situation more sympathetically than his own despairing family:

Alone in the wilds of Yorkshire, with few books, little to do, no prospects, and wretched pay, with no society congenial to his better tastes, but plenty of wild, rollicking, hard-headed, half-educated manufacturers, who would welcome him into their houses, and drink with him as often as he chose to come – what was this morbid man, who couldn't bear to be alone, to do?

Branwell's sisters were not natural conversationalists, and although their lives touched on different social spheres, they do not appear to have engaged anywhere except within their own family circle. During her time at Roe Head School, Anne Brontë formed a friendship with a pupil who was several years younger than her called Ann Cook, but the friendship does not appear to have survived outside school.

Emily Brontë appears to have been the only member of her family who never taught in the Sunday school and to have had little involvement with the villagers throughout her life. In her preface to the 1850 edition of Emily's *Wuthering Heights*, Charlotte wrote:

ABOVE *'She is good – she is true – she is faithful and I love her,' wrote Charlotte of her long-standing friend Ellen Nussey in a letter to W.S. Williams in 1850, answering a question of his about the 'infrequency of sincere attachments amongst women'. Literary fame brought Charlotte into contact with writers such as Elizabeth Gaskell and Harriet Martineau, producing new friendships, although as her letter to Williams indicates, she continued to value her old friends. This photograph shows Ellen Nussey in old age.*

ABOVE *Mary Taylor was from a similar social level to Ellen Nussey, although her home background was very different. It was from her upbringing that Mary developed her independent thinking and radical spirit. Mary emigrated to New Zealand and set up a shop. The business was very successful and she returned to England in 1860 with enough money to build a house and live independently. Mary published articles on women's rights and a novel, MISS MILES (1890).*

Though her feeling for the people round was benevolent, intercourse with them she never sought; nor, with very few exceptions, ever experienced. And yet she knew them: knew their ways, their language, their family histories; she could hear of them with interest, and talk of them with detail, minute, graphic, and accurate; but with them, she rarely exchanged a word.

Charlotte's lifelong friendships with Ellen Nussey and Mary Taylor, whom she met, along with Mary's younger sister Martha, in 1831 when they all became pupils at Miss Wooler's school at Roe Head, were unique among the sisters. Ellen and Mary both came from wealthier backgrounds than Charlotte, but while the Nusseys were a well-connected 'county' family, conservative in their politics, Mary and Martha were the daughters of Joshua Taylor, an outspoken manufacturer and banker with radical political opinions.

When not at school, Ellen and Mary lived within walking distance of each other, and with a shared network of relatives and friends, they could easily keep in touch. For Charlotte, living almost twenty miles away at Haworth, letters became the primary means of communication. At this period postage charges were levied on each sheet of paper used, and before 1840, were usually paid by the recipient. This meant that paper had to be used sparingly, and to avoid the necessity of starting a new sheet, the letter was often turned and the writing continued at right angles across the original letter. Ellen in particular was fond of sending such 'crossed' letters to ensure that the recipient got the best value for their money. Visits between the friends were often difficult to arrange, partly because of the lack of available transport in Haworth and partly because family obligations often frustrated their carefully laid plans. When the railway came to Keighley in 1847 matters were greatly improved, leaving only the four miles between Keighley and Haworth still to be travelled, either on foot or by hiring a covered cart or gig.

Charlotte made several visits to the Taylor family home, the Red House at Gomersal. Many years later when she came to write *Shirley* she portrayed the lively Taylor family as the Yorkes. On reading the novel, Mary's brother Joe remarked that 'she had not drawn them strong enough', while Mary commented: 'What a little lump of perfection you've made me!'

Mary Taylor told Elizabeth Gaskell how in the days before her celebrity, Charlotte regarded literary fame as a 'passport to the society of clever people', and certainly after the publication of *Jane Eyre*, the range of Charlotte's correspondents expanded to include several well-known authors of the day. By the time of her second of several visits to London, where she would stay at the home of her publisher George Smith, all her sisters were dead, and she sadly recalled how: 'Emily would never go into any sort of society herself, and whenever I went I could on my return communicate to her a pleasure that suited her, by giving the distinct faithful impression of each scene

I had witnessed. When pressed to go, she would sometimes say, "What is the use? Charlotte will bring it all home to me."'

Charlotte resisted Smith's attempts to show her off in London literary circles, although she did take advantage of the opportunity to meet the novelist W.M. Thackeray. Others whom Charlotte met in London and maintained a correspondence with included the author and reviewer G.H. Lewes and Harriet Martineau. Of the other friendships made in the last few years of Charlotte's life, one of the most rewarding was with the novelist Elizabeth Gaskell. Following their meeting at the Windermere residence of Sir James Kay-Shuttleworth in 1850, they corresponded and visited each other's homes, remaining friends until Charlotte's death five years later.

The excitement and stimulus of visits to London usually left Charlotte physically and mentally exhausted, however, and remained in sharp contrast to everyday life at Haworth Parsonage. Letters from friends were eagerly awaited and provided a lifeline to the outside world. In a letter to W.S. Williams written shortly after Anne's death, Charlotte wrote:

> The fact is, my work is my best companion – hereafter I look for no great earthly comfort except what congenial occupation can give – For society – long seclusion has in a great measure unfitted me – I doubt whether I should enjoy it if I might have it. Sometimes I think I should, and I thirst for it – but at other times I doubt my capability of pleasing or deriving pleasure. The prisoner in solitary confinement – the toad in the block of marble – all in time shape themselves to their lot.

Like the heroines in their own novels, the Brontë sisters were outsiders all their lives. Although accounts of their physical isolation have often been exaggerated, there can be little doubt that the Brontës were socially isolated at Haworth. Their seclusion, however, was not one that made itself felt, for it was shared amidst the intelligent companionship of an intensely close-knit family circle.

THE
BRONTË
LEGACY

LEFT *Upper Ponden, Haworth Moor, under a full moon.*

ABOVE *The Alcomden Stones on Stanbury Moor.*

MRS GASKELL AND THE BRONTË BIOGRAPHERS

Sometime, it may be years hence – but if I live long enough, and no one is living whom such a publication would hurt, I will publish what I know of her, and make the world (if I am but strong enough in expression,) honour the woman as much as they have admired the writer.

ELIZABETH GASKELL, letter to George Smith, 31 May 1855, two months after the death of Charlotte Brontë

When the first of the Brontë novels, *Jane Eyre*, was published in 1847, arousing a great deal of excitement and speculation regarding the identity of its author, Currer Bell, the novelist Elizabeth Gaskell, then at the start of her career, was one of the book's many fascinated readers. By 1850 a rumour that the notorious Currer Bell was actually a parson's daughter, living in a remote Yorkshire village, had reached her. In a letter she wrote of how she 'should like to hear a great deal more about her, as I have been so much interested in what she has written. I don't mean merely in the story and mode of narration, wonderful as that is, but in the glimpses one gets of *her*, and her modes of thought, and, all unconsciously to herself, of the way in wh she has suffered. I wonder if she suffers *now*.'

The meeting of the two novelists for the first time in August of that year at the summer residence of Sir James and Lady Kay-Shuttleworth, at Windermere was momentous. It not only resulted in a friendship that would last the remaining five years of Charlotte's life but would

also produce one of the most popular biographies ever written. Mrs Gaskell immediately dashed off accounts of the meeting to friends, spiced with snippets of information she had gathered partly from Charlotte herself but mainly from her gossipy hostess, Lady Kay-Shuttleworth.

Immediately after Charlotte's death spurious obituary notices began to appear in the press. Acting on a suggestion made by Charlotte's friend Ellen Nussey, Mr Brontë wrote to Elizabeth Gaskell, requesting her to write an account of his daughter's life. Aware of the great public interest in Charlotte's life, he realized that inevitably someone would undertake a biography and it was his hope that an authorized account, written by his daughter's sympathetic friend, would put paid to some of the more speculative and fanciful stories about the Brontë family that were appearing in the press. Mr Nicholls, while not entirely approving of the proposed biography, promised to help in any way he could, and soon Mrs Gaskell was setting about her task with enthusiasm. She made contact with many of those who had known Charlotte, and a year after agreeing to write the biography was able to inform Ellen Nussey that she believed she had 'been everywhere where she ever lived, except of course her two little pieces of private governess-ship'.

The Life of Charlotte Brontë was published in two volumes in March 1857, just two years after Charlotte's death. The frequent charges against the Brontë novels of 'coarseness' and brutality had been uppermost in Mrs Gaskell's mind and her biography set out to explain them

away. Her determination to show the extent of Charlotte's sufferings meant that other personalities were thrown into a harsh light, including Charlotte's father and brother. In describing Patrick Brontë as 'a wayward eccentric wild father' and using exaggerated accounts of Patrick's eccentricities in the *Life* to emphasize the peculiarities of Charlotte's upbringing, she overlooked the good he had done in Haworth over his forty-one years there. Charlotte emerges from the pages of the *Life* as a shining example of Victorian femininity. While Branwell's passion for Mrs Robinson is recounted in detail as the story that 'must be told', Charlotte's own love for her married Belgian schoolmaster is suppressed. Elizabeth Gaskell presents the Brontë sisters as living in a godforsaken village with only a

half-mad father, a debauched brother and a few surly neighbours for company. By showing the Brontës' lives in this light, she suggests that it was only natural that the Brontë novels would depict wild, eccentric characters.

After dispatching the last sheets of the work to the publisher, George Smith, Mrs Gaskell set out on a holiday to Rome. Initially, the biography was well received, but Mrs Gaskell does not appear to have foreseen that her novelist's instinct to tell a good story would lead her into trouble. Lady Scott, formerly Mrs Robinson, the wife of Branwell's employer at Thorp Green Hall, resented being portrayed as the 'bold and hardened' woman who had seduced Branwell and 'who not only survives, but passes about in the gay circles of London society, as a vivacious, well-dressed, flourishing widow'. Arriving home several weeks later, Mrs Gaskell found that further publication of the *Life* had been halted following a threatened libel action from Lady Scott. Apologies had been inserted in *The Times* and *The Athenaeum* on Mrs Gaskell's behalf and all unsold copies of the book had been withdrawn. 'I *did so try* to *tell the truth*', Mrs Gaskell wrote to Ellen Nussey, '& I believe *now* I hit as near the truth as any one *could* do. And I weighed every line with all my whole power & heart, so that every line should go to it's great purpose of making *her* known and valued, as one who had gone through such a terrible life with a brave & faithful heart.'

An expurgated version of the biography was called for. This eventually appeared as the third edition, 'Revised and corrected'. As Mrs Gaskell began the task of revision, protests came from all sides. Friends of William Carus Wilson, founder of the Clergy Daughters' School at Cowan Bridge, also threatened a libel action over her assertion that the school had been Charlotte's model for the infamous Lowood Institution in *Jane Eyre*. A battle in the newspapers took place, with Mr Nicholls joining the fray and defending his wife's depiction of the school. In a letter written to Ellen Nussey from New Zealand, Mary Taylor remarked: 'You must be aware that many strange notions as to the kind of person Charlotte really was will be done away with by a

OPPOSITE A portrait of Charlotte painted after her death by J.H. Thompson, a friend of Branwell's who knew Charlotte personally.

BELOW A photograph of Branwell's lost portrait of his sisters, known as the 'gun group'. The portrait depicted, from left to right, Anne, Charlotte, Branwell and Emily. Branwell is holding a gun and a brace of game birds lies on the table before him. Except for the figure of Emily, the painting was destroyed by Mr Nicholls who considered the other portraits to be poor likenesses.

knowledge of the true facts of her life … As to the mutilated edition that is to come, I am sorry for it. Libellous or not, the first edition was all true.'

Despite all the controversy surrounding the biography, a little knowledge of the Brontës' lives went a long way towards changing attitudes to their fiction. That Mrs Gaskell succeeded is made clear by the response of Charles Kingsley, who confessed to having been 'disgusted' by Charlotte's novel *Shirley*. After reading the *Life*, he complimented Mrs Gaskell on having 'given us the picture of a valiant woman made perfect by sufferings' and added that he would 'now read carefully and lovingly every word she has written'. Mrs Gaskell must also have taken comfort from the verdict of Charlotte's father, who despite the inaccuracy of his own portrayal, wrote: 'my opinion, and the

reading World's opinion of the "Memoir," is, that it is every way worthy of what one Great Woman, should have written of Another, and that it ought to stand, and will stand in the first rank of Biographies, till the end of time.' Although he recognized that Mrs Gaskell was primarily a novelist, he considered that she had 'not only given a picture of my dear daughter Charlotte, but of my dear wife, and all my dear children … The picture of my brilliant and unhappy son is a masterpiece.'

THE BRONTË BIOGRAPHERS

Although *The Life of Charlotte Brontë* appears to have satisfied many of those who had known the Brontës, Branwell's friends did not agree and put pen to paper in his defence. In *Pictures of the Past* (1879), Francis Grundy gave his own version of events, while at the same time emphasizing his own importance in Branwell's life. Francis Leyland, brother of Branwell's sculptor friend Joseph Bentley Leyland, felt that accounts of Branwell's life had 'been written by those who have some other object in view'. He challenged Mrs Gaskell's portrait of Branwell in his own two-volume account of the Brontës' lives, *The Brontë Family with Special Reference to Patrick Branwell Brontë* (1886).

Branwell's image, perpetuated by the many Brontë biographers following on from Mrs Gaskell, was one of alcoholism and failure. It was not until the 1960s that biographers were prepared to take a more sympathetic look at his life. In 1960 the first of two well-known biographies, Daphne du Maurier's *The Infernal World of Branwell Brontë*, appeared. Daphne du Maurier, like many of those who have written about the Brontës, was a novelist. Winifred Gerin's *Branwell Brontë* appeared in the following year. Rather than just portraying Branwell as bringing nothing but misery into his sisters' already miserable lives, both books stressed his innovatory role in all the Brontës' childhood activities and went on to consider his own creative output. Gerin, one of the most respected of the Brontë biographers, was also one of the few who believed Branwell's version of events in the Mrs Robinson affair. Although recent research suggests that her instinct was right, she undermined the credibility of her work by manipulating the evidence to support her theory.

Anne, the youngest and least appreciated member of the Brontë family, had to wait until 1959 before a book-length study of her life appeared in print. This was Winifred Gerin's *Anne Brontë*. Gerin cornered the market in Brontë studies, while her husband, John Lock, co-authored *A Man of Sorrow* (1965). This book considered Patrick Brontë's positive influence not only on the lives of his children but on his parish, where his duties had encompassed civil order, social welfare and health reform.

Interest in the Brontës had usually been focused on Charlotte, but by the end of the nineteenth century it was Emily's turn to be acknowledged as the greatest genius of the Brontë family. The first biography of Emily, written by Mary Robinson, appeared in 1883. Unlike her sister Charlotte, Emily had not formed friendships and wrote few letters. Apart from her only novel, *Wuthering Heights*, a handful of poems and some diary fragments, little source material relating to her has survived. A lack of biographical sources has not, however, prevented biographers from rushing to fill in the gaps and read the fiction as autobiography. Emily's solitary nature has allowed a great deal of scope for artistic licence.

There has been a strong tendency amongst biographers to describe in detail incidents that may well have never happened and generally embellish their accounts of the

Brontës' lives. This fictionalized type of writing has been called the 'Purple Heather School' of Brontë biography. The following sample is taken from Virginia Moore's *The Life and Eager Death of Emily Brontë* (1936):

> Charlotte had gone out and searched the blackened slopes for one spray of beloved heather. She found just one, doubtless in some fissure under a hill, protected from the wind. Its bells were not so very withered, and she brought it back to Emily. But Emily was already withdrawn; she was remote; she was far. She did not recognize her favourite flower.

This particular book serves as a cautionary reminder to other biographers: whatever the merits of Virginia Moore's work, her book is best remembered for the fact that she misread the title in a poetry manuscript by Emily, 'Love's Farewell', as 'Louis Parensell', and jumped to the conclusion that this must have been the name of Emily's secret lover.

In recent years the trend has been to cast aside the romantic mythology of the Brontës in order to write about them. This has been the approach taken by Juliet Barker, author of *The Brontës* (1994). In her words:

> Unlike their contemporaries, we can value their work without being outraged or even surprised by the directness of the language and the brutality of the characters. It is surely time to take a fresh look at the Brontës' lives and recognize them for who and what they really were. When this is done, I believe, their achievements will shine brighter than before.

A winter sunset over fields at Stanbury.

AFTER THE BRONTËS

Little by little, through the researches of this person or that, we have learned more and
more of the Brontës, and on the other hand, their one-time belongings are becoming
more and more scattered ... Unless a systematic effort be soon made to gather them
together, I fear the carrying out of the scheme for a museum will become impossible ...
A necessary preliminary to all this is the establishment of a Brontë Society.

W.W. YATES, *The Dewsbury Reporter*, November 1893

After the death of Patrick Brontë in 1861 and the sale of the contents of Haworth Parsonage, people who had purchased items at the sale were increasingly sought out by collectors and persuaded to part with their treasures. There was a growing sense among Bronte enthusiasts of the need to gather together and preserve the surviving possessions of the Brontës before the opportunity was lost for ever.

When the copyright in the Brontë novels expired in 1889, cheap editions of the works became readily available. This led to an increased interest in the lives and works of the three sisters. In the autumn of 1893 a proposal was made for the foundation of a society to promote the study of the works of the Brontës, and to collect and preserve what remained of the family's personal belongings. Shortly before Christmas in that year a small group of enthusiasts founded the Brontë Society. Many literary societies founded in this period did not survive, but the dedication and enthusiasm of its early members held the Brontë Society together, and its reputation spread far beyond the West Riding of Yorkshire where it had originated.

THE FIRST BRONTË MUSEUM

The society was founded in a period of active collecting of Brontëana, and many of the important manuscripts changing hands would eventually end up in America. There was still, however, one large collection to be found not so very far from Haworth. This had belonged to Martha Brown, a valued servant in the Brontë household, and consisted of drawings and paintings, inscribed copies of the novels and many of the sisters' personal belongings. The collection had remained virtually intact until Martha's death in 1880 and then passed to her five surviving sisters.

Part of this collection came up for sale in 1886, when the effects of the late Benjamin Binns were sold at Saltaire. The sale included forty-four lots of Brontë items that had passed from Martha Brown to Binns' wife, Ann, her elder sister. Eventually, Francis and Robinson Brown, Martha's cousins, acquired many of the lots from their original purchasers at the sale. In 1889 the enterprising Brown brothers opened the first museum of Brontë relics above their refreshment rooms in Haworth's Main Street. The venture was not a success, and the brothers moved to Blackpool, taking their Brontë collection with them. An attempt to display items at the Chicago Exhibition and then sell them on to rich Americans also failed. The newly formed Brontë Society hoped to buy the collection, but the asking price of £500 was far beyond its means. However, in a further disappointing attempt to dispose of the collection at Sotheby's in 1898, many of the 177 lots failed to find a bidder. Representatives of the Brontë Society were among those present, and they carried away Emily's watercolour of Anne's dog Flossy for the sum of £12. The society also acquired many other important drawings and paintings at the sale, some for as little as a few shillings each, and purchased the remaining items many years later from Francis Brown's daughter.

This was the society's first major purchase. Many other items were offered as loans, and eventually the society had assembled sufficient material to open a small museum. A room was secured over the Yorkshire Penny Bank in Haworth to display the collection, and on 18 May 1895 the Brontë Museum was officially opened. The day was an important occasion in Haworth and many people travelled from all over the country to be present at the opening.

In the following summer months nearly ten thousand people visited the small museum, among them Charlotte's close friend Ellen Nussey. The manuscripts of Charlotte's novels *Jane Eyre* and *Villette* were loaned by her publisher, Smith, Elder & Co., adding significantly to the museum's attraction.

From 1895, the society issued its own publications, encouraging research into the Brontës' works and lives. Social events also proved popular. Excursions to places with Brontë associations became an annual event and have continued to the present day.

In November 1897 Ellen Nussey died, aged eighty. Although she was never actively involved with the Brontë Society, her loss was keenly felt as a severance of one of the few surviving direct links with the Brontës.

As the society's collection of Brontëana grew, concern was expressed over its possible fate in the event of the society's demise, and after consideration, steps were taken for incorporation of the society. This would offer the society legal status. The charter of incorporation was granted in 1902 and the society became a company limited by guarantee, not having capital divided into shares.

ABOVE *The Brontë Society opened its first museum on the upper floor of the Yorkshire Penny Bank, now the Tourist Information Centre, at the top of Haworth's Main Street. The museum remained here for thirty-three years.*

Interest in the Brontës Grows

In the period of uncertainty leading up to the First World War, another link with the Brontës was lost when Charlotte Brontë's husband, Arthur Bell Nicholls, died in 1906, having survived Charlotte by fifty-one years. The Brontëana with which Nicholls had been unwilling to part during his lifetime was sold at Sotheby's in 1907. The society issued an appeal to its members for donations, and these made possible the purchase of a number of items at the sale. The Brontë Society acquired further items when the remainder of the Nicholls collection was sold in 1914 after the death of Mr Nicholls' second wife, Mary.

In 1913 four letters written by Charlotte Brontë to her Belgian professor, Monsieur Heger, were published in *The Times*. Charlotte's relationship with Heger had intrigued Brontë scholars for years. The publication caused great excitement and overshadowed other society concerns in that year.

Following the First World War, filmmakers made serious attempts to re-establish the British film industry, which was threatened by a flood of imported American films. The new films were often based on literary classics, with the British landscape predominating. One such attempt, billed as 'Emily Brontë's Tremendous Story of Hate', was the Ideal Film Company's silent production of *Wuthering Heights*. It was filmed in the Haworth area, with the Old Hall featuring as Wuthering Heights and Kildwick Hall in Keighley serving as Thrushcross Grange. A great effort was made to ensure the film's authenticity and a Brontë Society representative, Jonas Bradley, suggested many of the locations for filming. Popularization through the media increased interest in the Brontës. During the 1920s, postcards showing the interior of Haworth Parsonage,

ABOVE *In 1920 the Ideal Film Company arrived in Haworth to make the first film adaptation of* WUTHERING HEIGHTS. *Crowds thronged Main Street to catch a glimpse of the leading actors, Milton Rosmer and Anne Trevor.*

RIGHT ABOVE *A postcard showing the dining room at Haworth Parsonage in the 1920s before the house became a museum. There are many tales of disappointed visitors from as far away as America arriving at the Parsonage only to be informed that 'the rectory is a private house and not on view'.*

RIGHT BELOW *Sir James Roberts purchased the Parsonage in 1928 and on 4 August 1928, thousands turned out for the opening of the Brontë Parsonage Museum. In handing over the title deeds to the Brontë Society, Sir James said: 'It is to me a somewhat melancholy reflection that I am one of the fast narrowing circle of Haworth veterans who remember the Parsonage family.'*

then still a private home, were made available for sale in an attempt to satisfy the curiosity of sightseers.

HAWORTH PARSONAGE FOR SALE

Since its foundation, the Brontë Society had hoped that one day it would be able to acquire Haworth Parsonage. In the years after Patrick's death when the Parsonage had served as the home to four of Patrick's successors and their families, the Parsonage could be an inconvenient home, for it had become a literary shrine and, despite the protective screening of high walls and a tall garden gate, the occupants suffered constant intrusions from the many persistent Brontë devotees who found their way to the house. By 1927 the Brontë Society's collection had outgrown the cramped conditions in the one-room museum in Main Street; and at this time, when the society's total cash assets amounted to less than fifty pounds, the Ecclesiastical Commissioners announced that they were prepared to sell the Parsonage for a sum of £3,000.

The Parsonage was purchased by Sir James Roberts, a local man who had made a fortune in the textile industry. Not only did he hand over the title deeds to the Brontë Society but he also contributed a further £1,500 towards the cost of setting the Parsonage up as a museum and library. On 4 August 1928 thousands of people arrived at Haworth to witness the official opening of the Brontë Parsonage Museum.

With the acquisition of the Parsonage, many owners of Brontëana were prompted to return items to their original home. The society's reputation was further enhanced by Henry Houston Bonnell's magnificent collection of Brontë manuscripts, drawings and books, which arrived from America as a bequest to the museum. The society now entered a new and prestigious phase of its existence.

The society was keen to recreate the appearance of the Brontës' home, but plans to make changes to the far-famed Parsonage have always aroused controversy. One of the society's earliest changes was made in 1933 and involved the removal of a bathroom added by John Wade in the late nineteenth century to create extra storage. The *Keighley News* reported to its readers: 'Visitors to Haworth Parsonage do not go to look at cupboards but to see relics of the Brontë family. It has been the proud boast of every rector of Haworth since the days of Mr Brontë that the bath has remained intact as Charlotte used it.' Of course there was no plumbing in the Parsonage in the Brontës' day, only a portable shower bath, which had been acquired by Charlotte and would have been used in the kitchen.

FROM HAWORTH TO HOLLYWOOD

As the dark days of the Second World War approached, the ever-growing popularity of the Brontës was marked by the release of MGM's *Wuthering Heights*, a much-romanticized adaptation of Emily's novel. The museum remained open during the years of the war, and admission figures remained steady despite the advent of petrol rationing. The dining-room ceiling was strengthened and the windows blocked up in anticipation of enemy action.

From the early 1940s onwards there was a dramatic rise in the number of visitors to the museum. The works of the Brontës were widely read during the war years, with cinema adaptations proving extremely popular. The year 1943 saw the release of *Devotion*, a film based on the Brontë story. The filmmakers evidently found the reality of the Brontës' lives too grim to present to wartime cinema audiences, and once again the true story was greatly romanticized. A popular film adaptation of *Jane Eyre* starring Orson

AFTER THE BRONTËS

LEFT, ABOVE AND BELOW *The Brontë Society's first museum above Haworth's Yorkshire Penny Bank and the Parsonage dining room in the 1930s, then housing the Bonnell Collection.*

ABOVE *Haworth's much-photographed Main Street.*

Welles and Joan Fontaine was released the following year. Visitor numbers to the Parsonage doubled to 20,986, and by 1947 they had reached 53,649.

In 1944 a plaque commemorating the Brontë sisters' achievements was placed in Poets' Corner at Westminster Abbey. It was finally unveiled in 1947 when the war was over. The simple plaque, dwarfed by the more imposing memorials to Burns and Shakespeare, bears a line from a poem by Emily: 'With courage to endure'.

THE HOME OF THE BRONTËS

The growing museum collection required storage and display space, and the increasing number of visitors to the museum gave the society cause for concern. The stone steps leading to the front door of the Parsonage had to be reset because the feet of thousands of visitors had caused them to subside by over three inches. The front door and the stairs leading from it provided the only means of entrance and exit, and this fact caused a great deal of congestion and inconvenience to visitors. The 1960s were a period of greater financial stability for the society, which allowed it to contribute to the restoration of Haworth Sunday School, in which Charlotte had taught. The rationing and financial restrictions in the aftermath of the Second World War made building work and renovations difficult, but an extension to the old Parsonage was finally completed in 1960.

The new building, not visible from the front of the Parsonage, meant that the research library, formerly housed in the Wade Wing and part of the museum tour, could now be used by researchers. The large room above this, which had provided cramped accommodation for the museum's custodian, Harold Mitchell, and his family, could be used as exhibition space. A new flat for the custodian was built behind the Parsonage, connected to it by a glass loggia. The new extension provided much-needed space, but did not please everyone: a letter printed in the *Times Literary Supplement* accused the Brontë Society of 'deplorable vandalism'.

A start had already been made on restoring the original part of the house, with the construction of a fireplace in Mr Brontë's study. The creation of the Bonnell Room in what had formerly been part of the custodian's accommodation freed the dining room for a display of original furniture. A fireplace was added to create a more homely effect, but the period feel of the room was somewhat spoilt by the use of modern wallpaper. At this time a contemporary range was built in the old kitchen. Following these dramatic alterations, the appearance of the museum changed little

over the next twenty years. The plate-glass windows added by Mr Wade in the 1870s were replaced with small, Georgian panes, restoring the façade of the Parsonage to its appearance in the Brontës' time.

In 1973, Yorkshire Television broadcast a new drama scripted by Christopher Fry, *The Brontës of Haworth*. The drama was superbly cast and fired the public imagination, leading to almost a quarter of a million people beating a path to the Parsonage door. In this decade work began on the creation of a new strong room to house the growing collections in environmentally stable and highly secure conditions, but the appearance of the Parsonage remained unchanged throughout these years.

The 1980s marked a period of radical change at the Parsonage. In 1982 the upper floor of the wing added by John Wade was knocked through to create a large exhibition space. During the museum's closed period in 1987, picture rails dating from the late Victorian period were replaced by dados. Period wallpapers, including one based on a design found in Charlotte's writing desk, were introduced in the original part of the house, and information gleaned from contemporary accounts and newspapers was reflected in a new arrangement of furnishings. Items without a Brontë association were removed from display, although a bed, based on a drawing by Branwell, was specially commissioned for Mr Brontë's bedroom. This allowed the creation of a Brontë bedroom where household linen and furniture could be displayed.

In the years since 1987 modern conservation techniques have been employed

throughout the museum; these include low lighting levels and temperature and humidity controls. Ultraviolet film and window blinds are used, and exhibits are regularly changed to minimize their exposure. The Brontë Parsonage Museum

OPPOSITE *The bed displayed in Mr Brontë's bedroom was based on the drawing by Branwell shown on page 43.*

ABOVE LEFT *A brass plaque in Haworth Church marks the site of the Brontë vault. It was placed there in 1882 through the generosity of Sydney Biddell, an admirer of the Brontë sisters.*

ABOVE RIGHT *The preserved steam railway at Haworth was used in the 1970 film adaptation of E. Nesbit's* THE RAILWAY CHILDREN, *and has become a great tourist attraction.*

houses the world's largest collection of Brontëana, and as a literary shrine, it is second only to Shakespeare's home at Stratford-upon-Avon. Caring for collections of international importance requires a careful balance between preservation and accessibility, and the Brontë Society continues to search for the best means of serving its membership and the thousands of museum visitors without risk to the Parsonage or its fragile contents. Since its foundation in 1893, the Brontë Society has evolved from a small group of enthusiasts mainly based in Yorkshire into a worldwide literary body. Today it continues to care for the family's former home and to carry out its founding aim: to collect, preserve, publish and exhibit material relating to the Brontës' lives and works, and make them known to a wider audience.

SELECT BIBLIOGRAPHY

ON THE BRONTËS

Alexander, Christine, *The Early Writings of Charlotte Brontë*, Basil Blackwell, 1983

Alexander, Christine and Sellars, Jane, *The Art of the Brontës*, Cambridge University Press, 1995

Allott, Miriam, *The Brontës: The Critical Heritage*, Routledge & Kegan Paul, 1974

Barker, Juliet, *The Brontës*, Phoenix, 1995

Gaskell, Elizabeth, *The Life of Charlotte Brontë*, Penguin, 1985

Glen, Heather, ed., *The Cambridge Companion to the Brontës*, Cambridge University Press, 2002

Hewitt, Peggy, *Brontë Country: Lives & Landscapes*, Sutton Publishing, 2004

Ingham, Patricia, *Authors in Context: The Brontës*, Oxford University Press, 2006

Knight, Charmian and Spencer, Luke, *Reading the Brontës: An Introduction to their Novels and Poetry*, The Brontë Society and The University of Leeds School of Continuing Education, 2000

Miller, Lucasta, *The Brontë Myth*, Jonathan Cape, 2001

ON HAWORTH

Emsley, Kenneth, *Historic Haworth Today*, Bradford Libraries, 1995

Kellett, Jocelyn, *Haworth Parsonage: The Home of the Brontës*, The Brontë Society, 1977

Lemon, Charles, ed., *Early Visitors to Haworth: From Ellen Nussey to Virginia Woolf*, The Brontë Society, 1996

Wood, Steven, *Haworth: 'A strange uncivilized little place'*, Tempus, 2005

INDEX

ACKNOWLEDGMENTS

ANN DINSDALE

Many of the photographs reproduced in this book are from the Brontë Parsonage Museum, and I would like to thank the Brontë Society for permission to use them.

I offer my best thanks to all those who have helped and supported me in various ways in the writing of this book: Sarah Barrett, my sister Susan Burke, Steve Cuff, Mrs Anne Dransfield, Jane Sellars, Stephen Whitehead and Steve Wood. I should like to express too my gratitude to Anne Askwith, editor of this book, and Ian Hunt, the designer. Last but not least, I would like to take this opportunity to pay tribute to the staff of the Brontë Parsonage Museum, past and present.

SIMON WARNER

I would like to thank the Brontë Society and staff at the Brontë Parsonage Museum for their unfailing welcome and kindness, and the following for permission to photograph their properties: Hall Green Baptist Chapel, Julie and Steve Brown, Sheila Hogan and Chris Hodkin, and Barbara Whitehead at the Brontë Birthplace.

PHOTOGRAPHIC ACKNOWLEDGMENTS

For permission to reproduce the images on the following pages, and for supplying photographs, the Publishers thank those listed below.

Pauline Barfield, Keighley Local Studies Library: 112

© The Brontë Society (photographs by Simon Warner): 1, 2, 13 above, 14, 15, 16, 19, 20, 23 right, 26, 27, 29, 31, 33 above, 34, 35, 37, 38, 39, 43, 44, 45, 46 left, 48, 49, 50, 52, 54, 55, 56, 57, 61, 62, 63, 64, 65, 66, 67, 68, 72, 75, 78 below, 79, 87, 92, 93, 97, 101, 102, 103, 105, 106, 107, 111 above, 113 below right, 117, 121, 122, 124, 126, 128–9, 130, 131, 132, 133, 135, 136 left, 137, 138, 139, 143, 144, 145, 149, 150, 151, 152, 154

Reproduced by kind permission of Mrs R. Trevor Dabbs: 142

Peter Kingston: 84

Eric Stoney: 113 above left

© Simon Warner: 10–11, 13 below, 17, 21, 22, 23 left, 24–5, 30, 32, 33 below, 36, 40, 41, 42, 46 right, 47, 51, 53, 58–9, 69, 70–71, 73, 74, 76–7, 78 above, 81, 82, 83, 89, 90–91, 95, 96, 98, 108–9, 111 below, 113 above right, 114, 115, 116, 118, 119, 120, 123, 125, 127, 136 right, 140–41, 147, 153, 155